Part of It

GRAPHIC MEMOIRS BY ARIEL SCHRAG

Awkward

Definition

Potential

Likewise

Part of It

FICTION BY ARIEL SCHRAG

Adam

Part of It

comics and confessions by

Ariel Schrag

A Mariner Original

MARINER BOOKS

HOUGHTON MIFFLIN HARCOURT

BOSTON NEW YORK 2018

The following stories were inspired by true events. However, names and identifying characteristics have been changed and due to the malleability of memory and the indulgence of artistic license, they should be considered fiction.

For information about permission to reproduce selections from this book, write to trade.permissions@hmhco.com or to Permissions, Houghton Mifflin Harcourt Publishing Company, 3 Park Avenue, 19th Floor, New York, New York 10016.

www.hmhco.com

Library of Congress Cataloging-in-Publication Data
Names: Schrag, Ariel, author.
Title: Part of it : comics and confessions / by Ariel Schrag.
Description: Boston : Mariner Books, 2018. | "A Mariner original" |
Identifiers: LCCN 2018017247 (print) | LCCN 2018021733 (ebook) | ISBN 9781328972460 (ebook) | ISBN 9781328972446 (paperback)
Subjects: LCSH: Schrag, Ariel—Comic books, strips, etc. | Graphic novels. | BISAC: COMICS & GRAPHIC NOVELS / Gay & Lesbian.
Classification: LCC PN6727.S287 (ebook) | LCC PN6727.S287 Z46 2018 (print) | DDC 741.5/973 [B]—dc23
LC record available at https://lccn.loc.gov/2018017247ISBN 978-1-328-97244-6

Printed in China

SCP 10 9 8 7 6 5 4 3 2 1

For Mellie

Yes... But what exactly do you mean by "Part of It"?

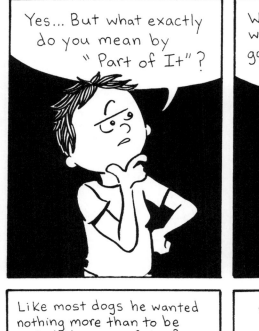

When my sister and I were teenagers my mom got a dog and named him Max.

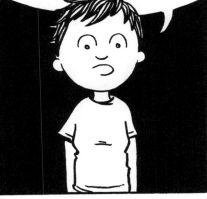

Because "Max" is literally the boringest name on earth you can give a dog, we took to calling him anything else.

Perch!

Brown Nose!

Possum!

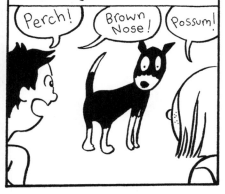

Like most dogs he wanted nothing more than to be included – part of the family. And so one name became:

Part of It

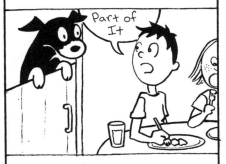

Or, more often, we began just announcing in his presence:

Not Part of It.

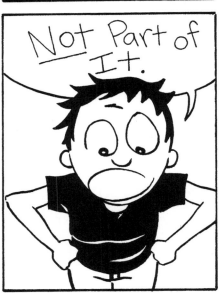

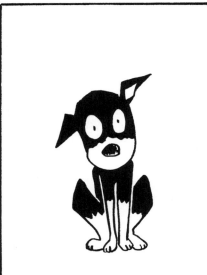

I'll admit there was a certain sadistic pleasure in this activity of which I'm not proud.

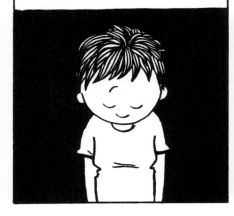

In Max's case "Part of It"– or lack thereof– was determined by species, but "Part of It" can refer to many things.

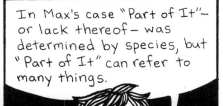

It can be the bond of friendship.

BEST FRIENDS

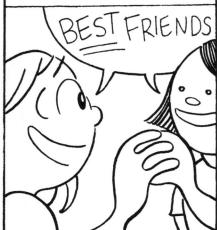

The security of family.

Take good care of your sister while we're gone!

Or the draw of a subculture.

DYKE RIGHTS

You can be born into "Part of It."

Baruch atah Adonai

Or you can attempt to cultivate it yourself.

Ultimately, "Part of It" is the feeling of belonging.

ARTS CAMP

But this belonging can be fragile and often requires the exclusion of others to sustain itself.

heeheeheeheehee

What feels so horrible about being excluded is the fear of a lack of self. Who are you without other people?

Can you even have an identity without other people? Who are you, really?

Well?

Contents

Jilly

1986 age 6

JILLY
Now let's play dogs!
OK!
Rrrowf Rowf
rowf rowf
rowf
rowf
Now let's play rape!
ok
You be the dirty old man who climbs through the window
No! I wanna be the girl, you have to be the man
fine
OK, ready, Jilly?
yeah

I don't really get how people have sex
I think they do it like this
But no, that doesn't make sense, 'cause the penis hangs down and the vagina is inside, they can't fit together that way
well how do you think they do it?
I think they must put their legs like this, see, then it can go in
maybe
Let's play something else
We could play this game I play with Ronica where one of us is a big fat emperor that has all of these girls come rub themselves in his crotch
nah
let's play horses!
OK!

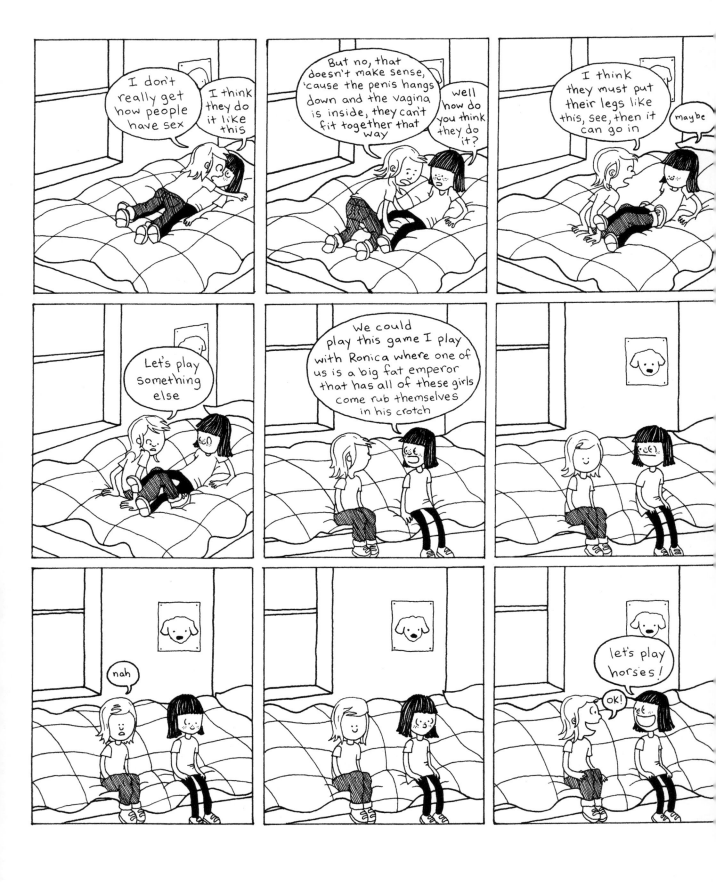

Hippies as Babysitters

1990 age 10

HIPPIES AS BABYSITTERS
AS
Keep Out
My Diary
Date 8/21/90
Dear Diary a lot has happend. My parents went away for the weekend in Sonoma.
It was the first time they'd ever been away overnight. I asked why me and Valerie didn't just come with them. Even if we don't drink wine, being too young, we could do something else.
This is just a thing Dad and I need to do. But don't worry, you'll have a babysitter, it will be fun! OK? It's going to be fun! We'll all have fun!
I wondered who our babysitter would be. I hoped it would be Isa, who lives in the house behind us. Isa is the most amazing, wonderful, beautiful person on earth.
5/7/90
Isa Isa Isa ISA Isa Isa Isa ISA Isa Isa ISA
But Mom said Isa is only thirteen, so can't babysit overnight.
Also I think her family's moving away.
chop chop
Our other main babysitter is Hilary.
Just a minute, I'm on the phone.
Hilary is the sort of person I would describe as having an active social life.
Ariel, get Valerie, and don't tell your mom, but we need to go to McDonald's right now so I can meet some friends, it's really important.

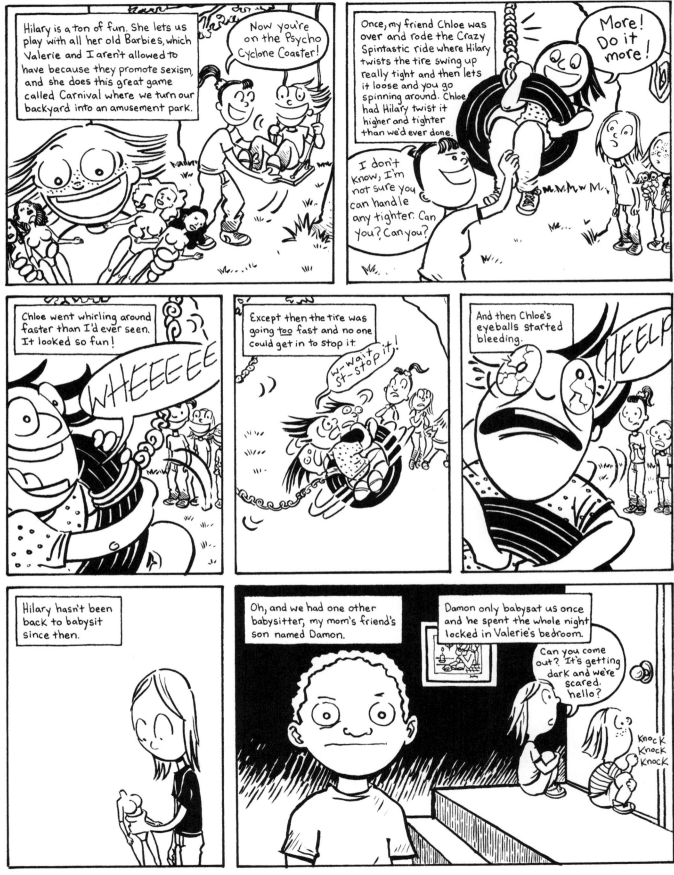

Hilary is a ton of fun. She lets us play with all her old Barbies, which Valerie and I aren't allowed to have because they promote sexism, and she does this great game called Carnival where we turn our backyard into an amusement park.

Now you're on the Psycho Cyclone Coaster!

Once, my friend Chloe was over and rode the Crazy Spintastic ride where Hilary twists the tire swing up really tight and then lets it loose and you go spinning around. Chloe had Hilary twist it higher and tighter than we'd ever done.

More! Do it more!

I don't know, I'm not sure you can handle any tighter. Can you? Can you?

Chloe went whirling around faster than I'd ever seen. It looked so fun!

WHEEEEEE

Except then the tire was going too fast and no one could get in to stop it.

w-wait st-stop it!

And then Chloe's eyeballs started bleeding.

HEELP

Hilary hasn't been back to babysit since then.

Oh, and we had one other babysitter, my mom's friend's son named Damon.

Damon only babysat us once and he spent the whole night locked in Valerie's bedroom.

Can you come out? It's getting dark and we're scared. hello?

Knock Knock Knock

The weekend was getting closer and I still had no idea who our babysitter was going to be. I don't think Mom and Dad did either.
You were supposed to take care of this, Frances.
Denie was happy to do it.
Denie is a crazy person.
So we won't go. I'm fine to not go. We don't need to go.
My mom had recently decided she needed extra help, so now we had a housecleaner named Kimberely who came every two weeks.
And then I discovered that Kimberely was going to be our babysitter!
it would just be for the weekend, and you're welcome to stay here in our bedroom. We'd pay you of course.
I'd love to! I love kids! My fiancé Stephen will be so excited!
The girls are really easy, they're happy to go to Live Oak Park across the street, we'll leave you money in case you want to go to the movies.
We'll have tons to do! It will be fun! My fiancé Stephen is great with kids.
Kimberely seemed really excited to be our babysitter for the weekend.
OK, great! I'm glad you can do it.
Yeah, definitely! I can't wait to tell my fiancé Stephen!
So, ah, it will just be you sleeping in the bedroom, not Stephen.
Right, of course!
I was excited too. I lay awake at night pretending I was a girl who was going to be babysat by a woman named Kimberely and her fiancé Stephen.

Finally, Friday arrived.
Have fun!
bye
bye!
bye!
As soon as our parents left, Kimberely told us that all the food in our house was toxic and the microwave was slowly killing us.
Bisquick
Triscuit
We need to get to the Farmers Market!
Then Kimberely's fiancé Stephen showed up at the door.
Stephen!
hey kids
We all went out to go to the market. Both Kimberely and Stephen are very devoted to the cause of peace and organic stuff. And everywhere we walked we met a friend who's fighting too.
US out of Iraq!
US out of Iraq!
Lucas! Brother. See you at the demo Sunday?
Of course! Peace!
Peace!
Janice, hi! This is Ariel and Valerie!
hello!
How's it going man, Peace!
Peace!
hi! I'm Ariel.
hey!

We met a man named Chris who was very interesting. He talked about all his long-lost loves he broke up with.
It's over with Eric. He's just not "in love anymore," it's like what Susan said to me all over again. Still not over that. I thought I could fall in love with John, but he's not interested.
why is he saying boys' names—
Shhh!
And we were angry when we saw a car that had pollution coming out so Chris shouted:
YOUR CAR IS EMITTING DEATH YOU FUCKING BITCH!
asshole
Then we ran into my friend Gemma and her parents. I felt cool and above it all in front of Gemma.
I'm Kimberely and this is my fiancé Stephen!
where are your parents?
They're not around anymore.
I pretended my parents were never coming back and this was my new life now.
That night Kimberely put on music and we all cooked dinner together.
I want to get up and jive!
Alive! Alive!
I'm just so happy, Stephen!
That's all I want in this world.

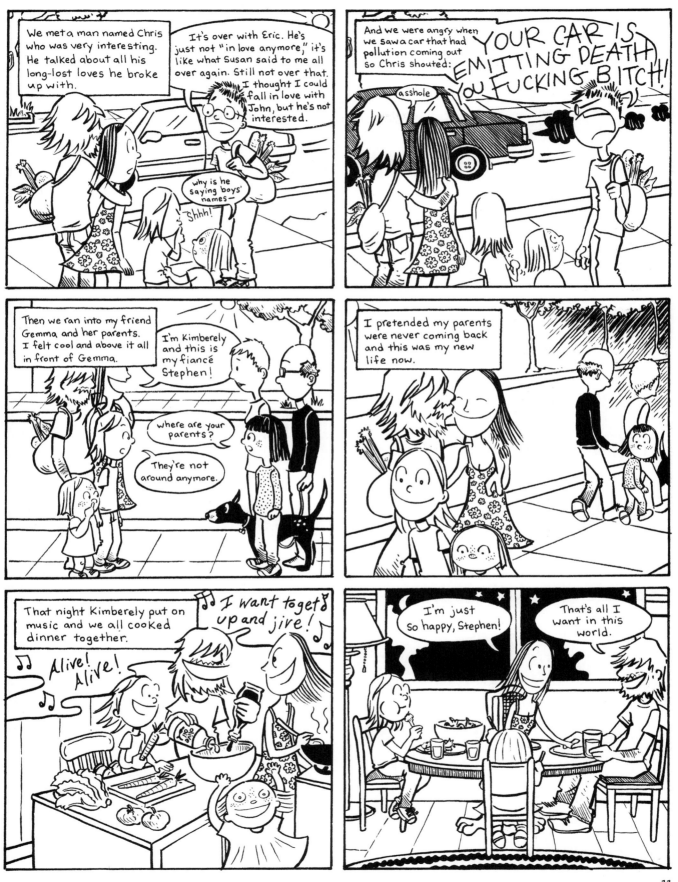

After dinner, Kimberely and Stephen wrestled around, playing like they like to do.
I should get the kids to bed now.
OK, I'll go upstairs and wait in our bed.
Stephen... I told you. We're not spending the night together here. Just me.
What?! Why not. They don't have to know.
Stephen
Stephen was not happy when he left. We felt really sad to see him go.
Stephen
It's OK. Stephen's just being Stephen. Do you want a story before bed?
The next day we hung out at Kimberely and Stephen's house. It was really cool.
Ariel and Valerie love to draw. You should show them what an amazing artist you are.
MARCH FOR PEACE AUG. 1ST.
Ashkenaz LIVE! $5
GILMA
GREEK THEATER
GULF WAR
Stephen was one of the best drawers I have ever seen in my life. He'd start out drawing something and I'd have no idea what it was going to be and then, suddenly, the whole thing would come together.
PEACE AUG. 1.
LIVE $5
GREEK THEATER

We had so much fun and even made a pyramid piggyback!
Eeeeek!
WHEEEE
WHOAAA
HaHa HaHa
I also realized Kimberely wears no underwear.
MARCH FOR PEACE
I saw when she jumped and picked up her skirt dancing.
I dreamed I saw the bomber planes
Turning into butterflies
MARCH FOR PEACE AUG. 1ST
LIVE MUSIC! $5
HAIGHT ASHBURY is love
It was starting to get dark when a bunch of friends came over. Something really important was happening.
Come on, get your sleeping bags, we're all camping out in People's Park as part of the protest.
Chris said Channel 5 is already on its way over.
No shit!
the sleep-in is tonight?
Fuck the sleeping bags, we should just lay out on some burlap sacks, let them really see us.
I'll fucking pepper spray them back, I will.
B-but Stephen, we have Ariel and Valerie tonight.
So what? We can come! I want to come!

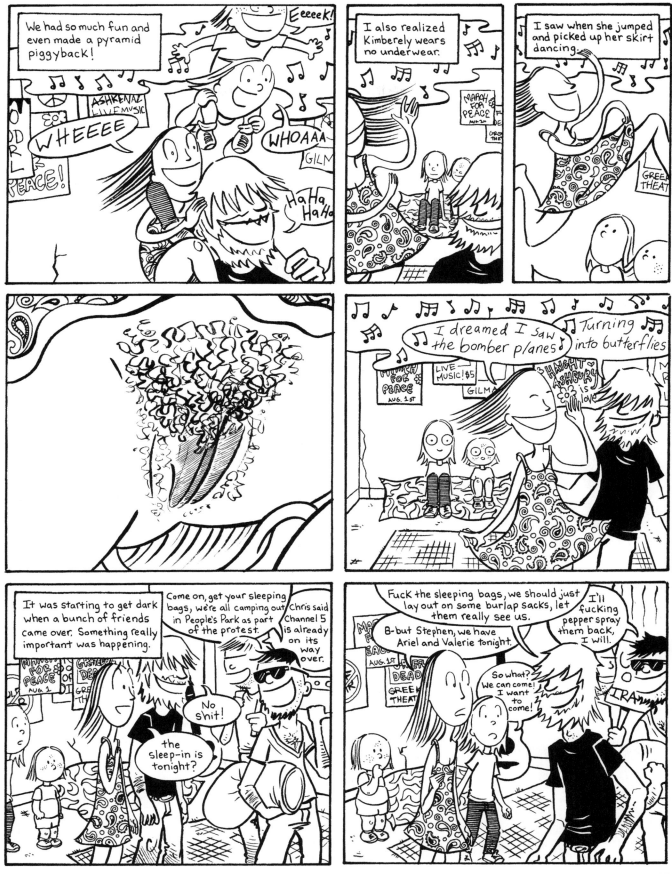

This one's a fighter! She wants to come!
We'll go to the next protest, but we have to go back to their house tonight.
So you go. I'm doin' the sleep-in.
NO BLOOD FOR OIL! NO BLOOD FOR
But you said you'd spend the weekend with us.
I'm doin' the sleep-in, if you're not with us, don't come.
But Stephen
Do you think I like that this is happening the night of the sleep-in? I don't want to miss it either!!
So bring the kids to the protest first and when it gets late go home.
But Valerie's too young...
So we'll get a babysitter for her! We have to go! Come on! We have to go!
I, I have to take the kids home. I just thought we could cook dinner together again...
We'll call Hilary! We can leave Valerie with her and all go to the protest! Let's just leave her with Hilary!
I don't wanna just stay and cook dinner again.
We're headin' out, see you at the park if you decide to come. Peace!
snf
wink
OUT OF IRAQ
Fine. I'll stay.
LIVE MUSIC! $5
MARCH FOR PEACE
WAR NO MORE
DROP BUSH NOT BOMBS
It's not so bad. We'll have fun!
It's fine.

We went back to me and Valerie's house.
Kimberely put on music, but nobody really seemed much in the mood for dancing.
We hadn't been to the Farmers Market that day, but still had some vegetables left in the refrigerator.
Just enough for a vegetarian lasagna casserole.
Flush
LASAGNA
Stephen? Stephen, could you come here and help?
LASAGNA
whuhuhh huhwhuhh nuhwhh uhh
Valerie! what's the matter?!
what's wrong?
I have diarrhea

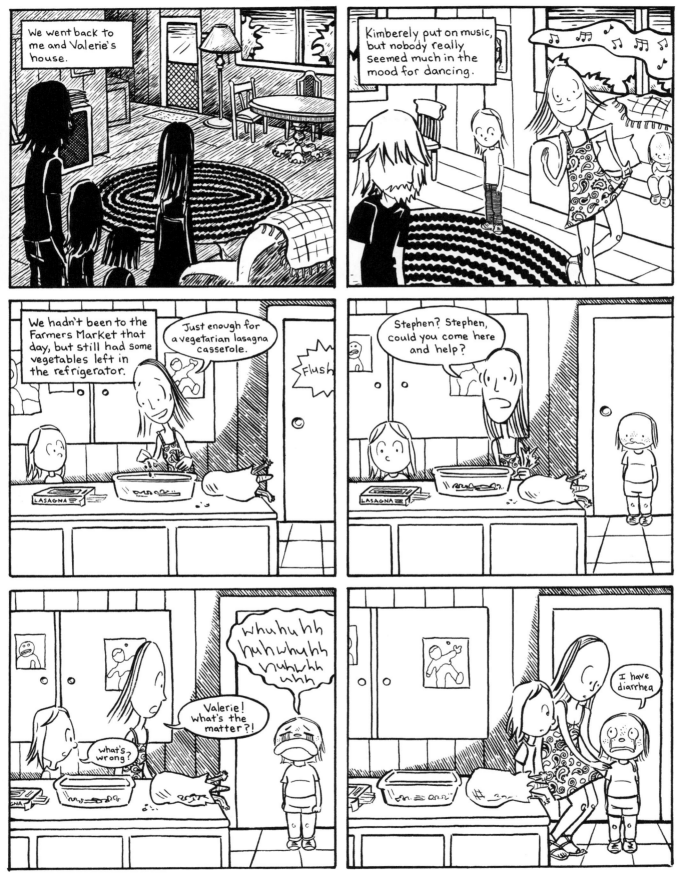

Do you want to go back to the bathroom? Is there something you usually do for this?
I have diarrhea
Kimberely got Valerie settled on the couch with a story, so I went upstairs to go play in my room by myself.
Stephen was in my parents' bedroom, lying on their bed, reading a book.
O. HENRY

I went in my room and played until dinner.
That night, I pretended I was an orphan who had been traveling through the woods for days and stumbled upon this deserted, empty house and sought shelter.
Date
When my parents came back we all went out to Fat Apples to celebrate.
Did you have fun?
Yeah! We met all these really cool people and almost went to a sleep-in in People's Park!
a sleep-in?
I got diarrhea!
I never saw Kimberely again. After my parents got back, Mom decided we don't need a housecleaner and that everyone who's a member of this family should do their part to keep the communal living space clean. As for babysitters, we've had a few others, but no one serious. Besides, I'm almost eleven and soon will be babysitting myself.
How old is Ariel getting to be now?
I can hardly wait.
Keep Out

Jilly II
1993 age 13

JILLY II
come on! we should do it!
yeah!
should we?
what if we get caught!
then we're all in it together! come on!
let's do it!
I'm nervous!
OK, we swear. If anyone gets caught, we were all in it together.
OK, who goes first
you do it
I don't want to do it
I'll do it

FUCK LUIS
The secretary was extremely shocked to find your message in the bathroom. She couldn't believe girls here had done it, but I told her I knew who it was.
Ronica, I expected. Lucy, I'm surprised. Ariel, I can understand.
why is Jilly here?
Of course all your parents will be notified, I hope you realize that, also—
what's Jilly doing here
why is Jilly here?
I don't know
Jilly, did you participate in the writing on the mirror?
No, but if I was there, I would have.
OK... Jilly, you may leave... and you four will have a thirty-minute detention after school.

Plan on the Number 7 Bus

1993 age 13

you got everything we need?
yeah
URBAN UTFIT
PLAN ON THE NUMBER 7 BUS
BYE MOM Ronica and me are taking the bus to Hope's house
hold on a minute
URBAN OUTFITTERS
Do you know how to take the bus to Hope's house? Has Ronica done it before?
No. But Hope gave us directions.
She gave us directions! We'll figure it out.
Well Hope lives up in Kensington on Russell, I think. So you'll want to take the number 7 bus up Spruce Street. Did she say her house is close to the bus stop?
Yes! she said it's a block away. I take the bus all the time. we're fine.
You never take the bus.
what?! I take the bus home from school like every day, and sometimes to school!
Gemma takes the bus. Not you.

oh my god! do you think your mom saw your hickey?!
Aaah! I don't know! After Jarred left yesterday she was like, "who was that?"!
Hee hee hee hee
URBAN OUTFITTERS
I can't wait for "Plan"! hee hee
I know!!
So I went to the movies with Gemma and Lucy and Saeed and people on Saturday-
you did? but-
-and we totally ran into Hope and Rosie!
wait! we totally don't know who could get on this bus, we should use the code names!
URBAN OUTFITTERS
ok, so I was with "Plaid"
Gemma = Plaid
and "Chicken"
Lucy = Chicken
hey, can I have a bite of your sandwich?
uh, no
Yummy Chicken sandwich, can I have some?
sure!

and I forget what we call all those other people. Anyway, so we ran into— "The Seaweeds."
Seaweed = flat
Hope + Rosie = flat
The Walls from Mother Fucking Hell! heeheeheeheee
URBAN OUTFITTERS
Wait! so then what happened?!
That's it.
oh my god! Did you know that on Friday, Jilly tried to come eat lunch with me and people! Saeed was like, "shouldn't you be eating lunch behind the dumpsters with Amy?"!
Yeah, Gemma was coming over to my house one day and Jilly was on the bus and she was like totally talking to this homeless guy!
URBAN OUTFITTERS

Yeah, I'm into punk music, I hang out on Telegraph, I think I've seen you there.
oh yeah?
Gemma doesn't come over to your house.
Gemma totally comes over to my house, you were THERE like last Thursday when she and Robbie came over!
Ew, remember how Robbie was sitting in that chair and Gemma was like in between his legs and when she got up he was like, "No, don't move" and like pushed her in closer?!
Ew! I know! I like went to the bathroom and when I went back in my room Gemma - I mean "Plaid," was sitting on the bed and Robbie was like Kneeling on the floor with his head like-
Gross, well you know what Kyle said he did with her-
Yeah, I know! I can't believe it...
ew, she's such a whore!
she's totally a slut.
hee, hee. Remember what happened after Gemma left?
SCRABBLE
MONOPOLY

God, Jarred is so fine. Do you think Hope will ever wear a bra?
URBAN
a baby training bra her mommy buys her with a little rosebud in the middle.
she's like fat and flat, what could be worse!
URBAN

OK, you guys, so I'm positive Ronica stuffs. She was reaching over to grab something and I saw through her sleeve and I'm like positive there was a shoulder pad in there.
I don't know...
She does seem a lot bigger all of a sudden.
and Robbie told me that Sam said that when he and Hope were going out they never even Kissed!
he probably tried and she was like—
ALIEN: ELIMINATE
URBAN OUTFITTERS
heeheeheeheeeheeeheeeheeehee
URBAN OUTFITT
Let's go over "Plan"!
Yes! She's gonna be totally humiliated.

OK, so we get to Hope- I mean "Sea-" No, "Kelp's" house. And she's probably listening to KMEL.
Hi guys!
SLOW JAM
and we're like, "Uh, can we change the radio station?"
Sure! to what?
Live 105! KITS!
rock?
SKREEE
Then I dump out my Urban Outfitters bag. Caboodles comes out, and Reals and Box.
URBAN OUTFITTERS
CABOODLES MAKE UP CENTER
TAMPAX TAMPONS
and I'm like, "Gosh, I need lip gloss for my chapped lips"
where is it?
and you pick up Real and go:
Ooooh, is this new? I think I saw it at Bancroft.
and I'm like:
No, it's from Urban, isn't it fresh?
Damn straight

Then I start rubbing my neck and I'm like:
uhhh, it hurts.
and you go: "Gimme Five"
SLAP!
and Hope is like:
what? what is it?
and I go, "you know" and show her others
and she says:
ALIEN: ELIMINATE!
CABOODLES MAKE UP CENTER
FITTERS
TAMPAX TAMPONS

heeheeheeheeeheeheeheeheeheeheeheeheehee
heh heh... so anyway, did you hear what Ms. Erikson said to Saeed and Luis on Friday? She was like, "I know where you guys go after school."
yeah
when were we supposed to get off?
and Gemma was like, "Saeed thinks he's so fresh 'cause he goes with someone from King," but she's met Becca and I've met Becca.
yeah...

URBAN
SKREEEEEE
WHOOOOOOSH

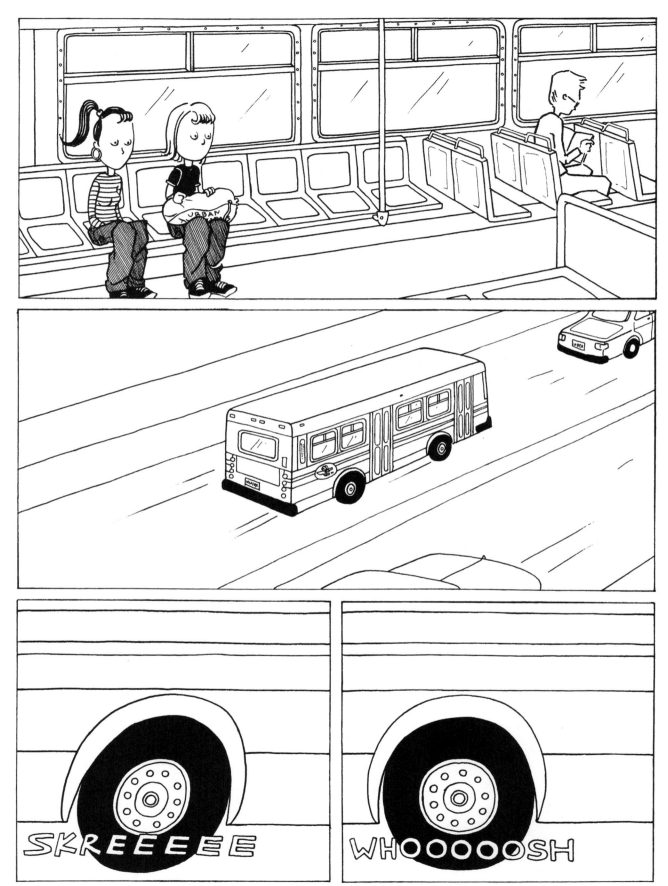

END OF THE LINE.
EVERYONE OFF.

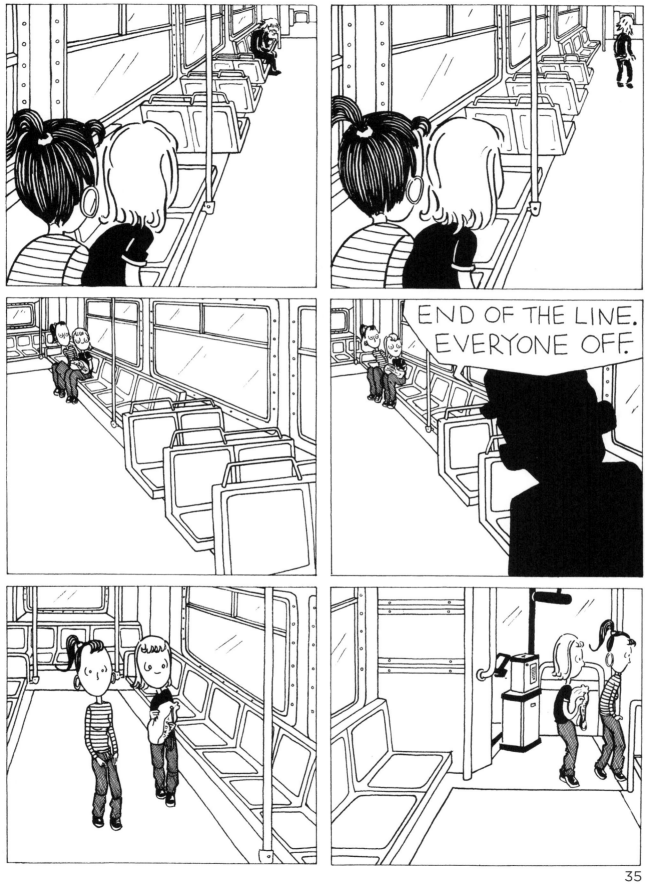

W-where are we?
I don't know

AC TRANSIT BUS SERVICE
URBAN
UTFITTERS

AC TRANSIT BUS SERVIC
URBAN OUTFITTERS
EL CERRITO STATION
AC T BUS ICE
EL CERRITO STATION
AC BUS VICE
URBAN FITTERS
I-I'm gonna call my mom.
me too
URBAN OUTFITTERS
ring ring ring
BELL
"Hello, you've reached..."
ring ring ring
"We're not home right now..."

PACIFIC BELL
URBAN
I am so scared
I am so scared
I am so scared
AC TRANS

Oh god I'm sorry I'm sorry I'm sorry
I'm sorry I'm sorry
OUTFITTERS
I'm sorry I'm sorry
URBAN OUTFITTERS
please please
URBAN OUTFITTERS
BELL
what is she doing? is she going to talk to them?! oh god please don't talk to them I'm sorry. I'm sorry.
URBAN OUTFITTERS
I just wish I was at Hope's house I wish I was at Hope's house.
Hope is good Hope is good Hope is good

oh God I'm sorry. I'm sorry. The Plan was fucked up. I know you intervened. Please, just let me be safe, just let me be safe.
URBAN OUTFITTERS
Ok I swear to God, I swear to myself. I'm making a pact. I am making a vow—
I CANNOT BE MEAN.
The days of the seaweeds, of Jilly, of everyone are over. Each time I say anything mean about anybody I bite and I bite hard and I stop and apologize. That is it. This is Final. There is no turning back.
I CANNOT BE MEAN. I CANNOT BE MEAN.
OUTFITTERS
I CANNOT BE MEAN I CANNOT BE MEAN
URBAN OUTFITTERS
ring ring
I CANNOT BE MEAN I CANNOT BE MEAN
hello?
I CANNOT BE MEAN I CANNOT BE MEAN
m-om

PACIFIC BELL
I CANNOT BE MEAN I CANNOT BE MEAN
E-El Cerrito. The end of the line. ...OK. Th-thanks
I CANNOT BE MEAN I CANNOT BE MEAN
BELL
I CANNOT BE MEAN I CANNOT BE MEAN
URBAN OUTFITTERS
I CANNOT BE MEAN I CANNOT BE MEAN
I CANNOT BE MEAN I CANNOT BE MEAN
I CANNOT BE MEAN I CANNOT BE MEAN
I CANNOT BE MEAN I CANNOT BE MEAN

I CANNOT BE MEAN I CANNOT BE MEAN
URBAN
TFITTERS
HONK
BAN
TTERS
I CANNOT BE MEAN!
I CANNOT BE MEAN!
URBAN
1945
I Knew this would happen. Ronica, I'm going to take you home.
OK
I CANNOT BE MEAN I CANNOT BE MEAN
URBAN
OUTFITTERS

HA HA! YOU'RE DUMB!
SHUT UP.
URBAN
I cannot be mean... I cannot be mean...
URBAN
I cannot...
URBAN
URBAN

Shit

1994 age 14

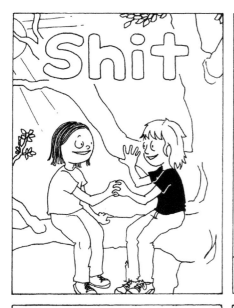

Shit

It was eighth grade and Samantha Curtis, the new girl, had become my best friend. I had recently been ostracized from the rest of the class by my former best friend, Ronica,

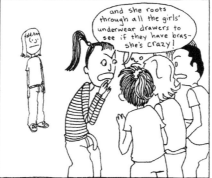

"and she roots through all the girls' underwear drawers to see if they have bras- she's crazy!"

and Samantha was like this cherub angel dropped from above, uninvolved and eager to be friends with anyone.

One weekend she invited me to go on a trip with her family on their houseboat. Me and my new best friend! It felt magnificent.

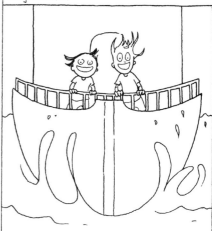

Her parents anchored the boat next to a large house of some of their friends. We would be staying there two nights. The parents would sleep in the house and Samantha and I would camp out in the boat.

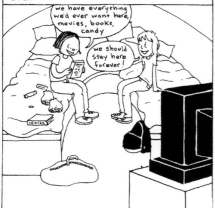

"we have everything we'd ever want here, movies, books, candy"

"we should stay here forever!"

when we went to go meet her parents for dinner with their friends up in the house, she pointed out the boat's toilet.

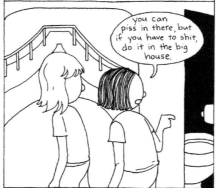

"you can piss in there, but if you have to shit, do it in the big house."

The fact that if I used her parents' friends' toilet it would be totally obvious that I was shitting was completely horrifying, and I decided that if I had to go I would just have to hold it until we got home.

After dinner the parents stayed around the table talking and Samantha and I adjourned to another room to play cards.

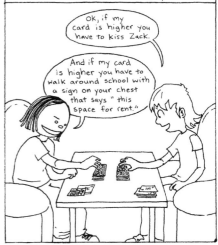

"Ok, if my card is higher you have to kiss Zack."

"And if my card is higher you have to walk around school with a sign on your chest that says "this space for rent.""

We stayed up really late watching "Stand By Me" and eating candy.

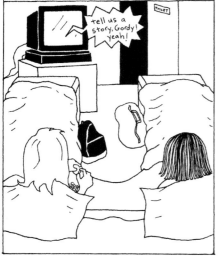

"tell us a story, Gordy! yeah!"

The next day we spent the afternoon running around and climbing trees in the woods behind the big house.

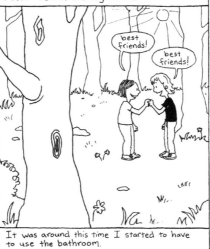

"best friends!"

"best friends!"

It was around this time I started to have to use the bathroom.

During dinner the pressure in my colon began to build. I told myself now was the time, I had to go now, we were in the house, all I had to do was politely excuse myself - but I could not do it. everyone would know. To make matters worse, one of the rounds I'd lost in the card game last night was that I had to eat all of Samantha's vegetables.

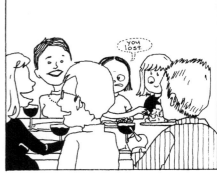

"you lost."

After dinner Samantha and I went back to the boat where we started another round of the card game. I was starting to sweat profusely and had to sit in a cramped, bent position. Still, the thought of interrupting the game to tell Samantha I had to "go up to the big house" seemed embarrassing beyond belief.

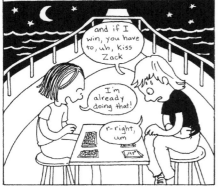

> and if I win, you have to, uh, kiss Zack

> I'm already doing that!

> r-right, um

Not to mention the fact that even if I got up the courage to tell Samantha, there was no way in hell I could face the parents' friends.

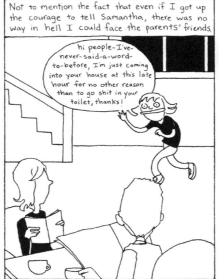

> hi people-I've-never-said-a-word-to-before, I'm just coming into your house at this late hour for no other reason than to go shit in your toilet, thanks!

Finally, I couldn't take it any longer. I broke down, gasped "I have to pee" and ran to the boat's toilet.

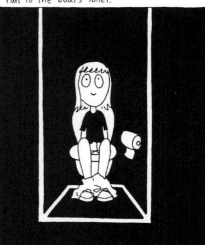

It was like an airplane toilet with no water and when I flushed, it appeared to start sucking the shit away, but scared that Samantha would note how long I was in there, I left before I could fully tell.

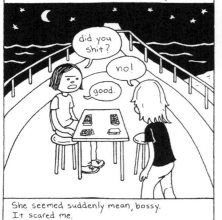

> did you shit?

> no!

> good.

She seemed suddenly mean, bossy. It scared me.

Later on, Samantha went up to the house to use the bathroom

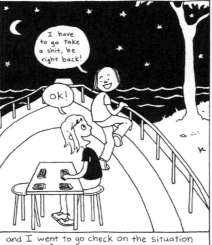

> I have to go take a shit, be right back!

> ok!

and I went to go check on the situation I had left.

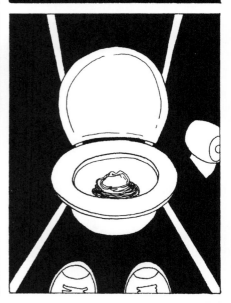

I tried flushing again, but this time it didn't budge. In a panic I wrapped my fist in toilet paper and tried shoving it down the hole.

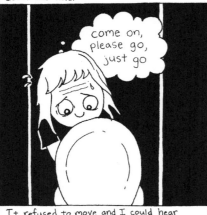

> come on, please go, just go

It refused to move and I could hear Samantha climbing back onto the boat.

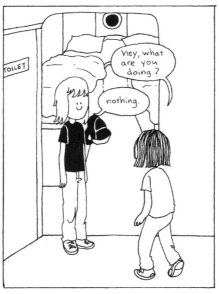

> hey, what are you doing?

> nothing.

We went into our sleeping room and started watching "Stand By Me" again.

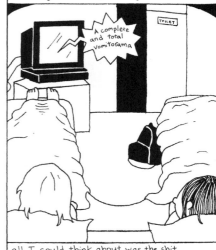

> A complete and total vomitorama

all I could think about was the shit.

The way I saw it, there were two possible outcomes.

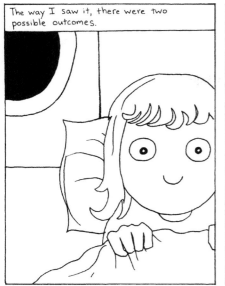

One. Samantha decides to go to the bathroom.

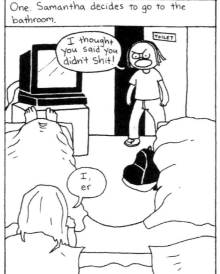

I thought you said you didn't shit!

I, er

Two. Her parents discover it the next morning.

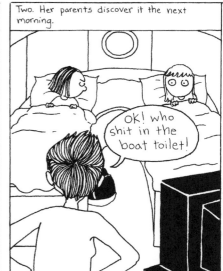

OK! who shit in the boat toilet!

The thought of either of these was death. But what could I do? How could I make my shit disappear?

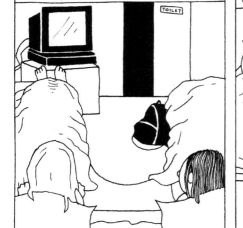

After thinking and thinking it was clear that there was only one solution. I was going to have to move my shit out of the toilet and into my backpack.

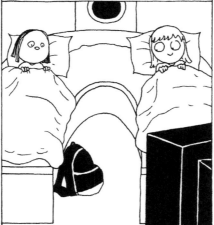

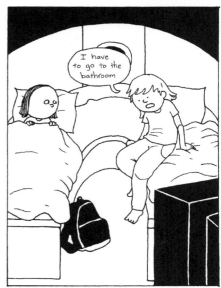

I have to go to the bathroom

I grabbed a wad of toilet paper and scooped up a ball of it covering this with more toilet paper.

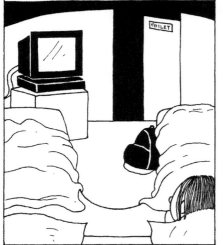

I put the ball in my pocket, grabbed more toilet paper, scooped up the rest, covered it with more toilet paper and put that into my other pocket.

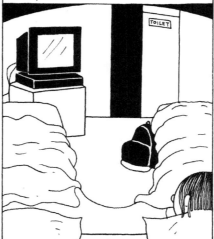

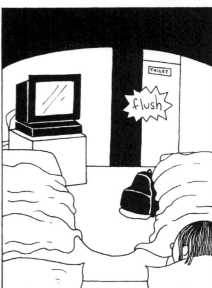

flush

49

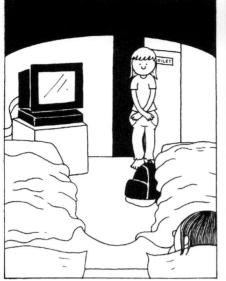

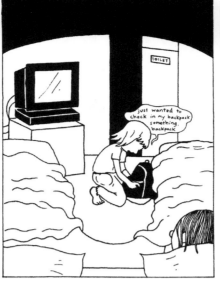

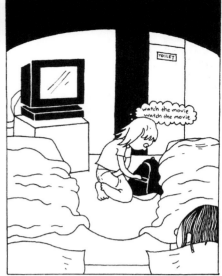

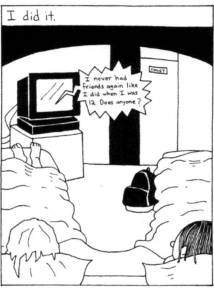

I did it.

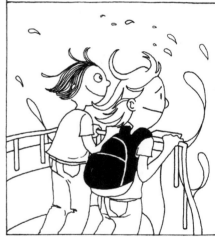

The next day I carried my backpack around with me everywhere. Maybe it looked weird, but the risk of leaving it unattended was too great.

We got back to the dock and Samantha's parents drove me home. Finally in my own house, I rushed to our bathroom and rid myself of the evidence forever.

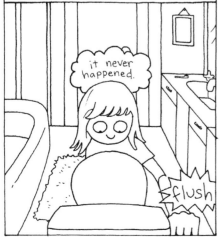

Two weeks later, Samantha dumped me for Ronica.

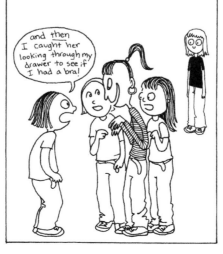

But in just one month we were graduating. And goddammit, I was ready for anything.

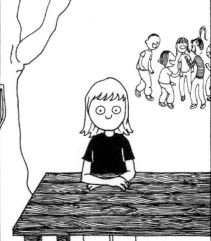

The Truth
1997 age 17

This comic was written during my junior
year of high school. It references a
series of graphic memoirs that I wrote
from 1995 to 1999, chronicling my
high school years.

fine.
well I mean honestly Ariel, you can't expect to just go and write and publish something like that when it blatantly says stuff about me. I mean, don't you even care!?
Of course I care! I mean obviously I don't wanna go and make you look bad - or whatever, but I mean, it's like... the truth.
Ok, we just need to think of a plan...
there's got to be some other way we can get around it...
um... you can tell people... uh...
it's a lie! yeah! I made it up for shock val—
You Realize you'll be receiving bags of my blood in the mail!
Look. you know how important the comic book is to me, I mean it's my life. writing it just isn't an option - that's why we like excessively talked about it before it happened and you knew I was going to write about you. and now just because you change your mind after what happened shouldn't mean that I'm suddenly not able to do what is like the most important thing to me.
you are so self-centered. so self-centered.
it's not self-centered if—
all you think about is yourself.
that is not true if—

totally self-centered.
If I was self-centered then I would have just gone and did it and expected to write about it without it even occurring to me what effect it would have but that's not what happened and I do care and it does matter what people think and that's why I made sure we talked about it before we had sex...
OK, we just have to think, there's gotta be some way I can still tell the story how it was but not have everyone know that it's you, uh, hmmm, OK...
OK, I'm getting it, you tell people, before the comic comes out, you tell them that the whole story in reality happened with that boy I went out with over the summer.
yeah, this'll work, you say that me losing my virginity was such an important event that I had to include it in the comic, but since the book only takes place in the school year and I never saw that guy after the summer it was easier to use that story with you who was already a prominent character in the book.
right?!? so that way, it's still the total truth to me but anyone you don't want to know you just tell them I couldn't deal with too many character and time changes and using you made it simple!
plausible... plausible...

so yeah we'll both tell that story to several people so it will circulate as well as you telling the specific people you don't want to know. Since it was just us it's not like there's any proof so there's no way people could find out it was really you.
yeah, it's definitely plausible.
fine.

Fight at the Gay Prom

1999 age 19

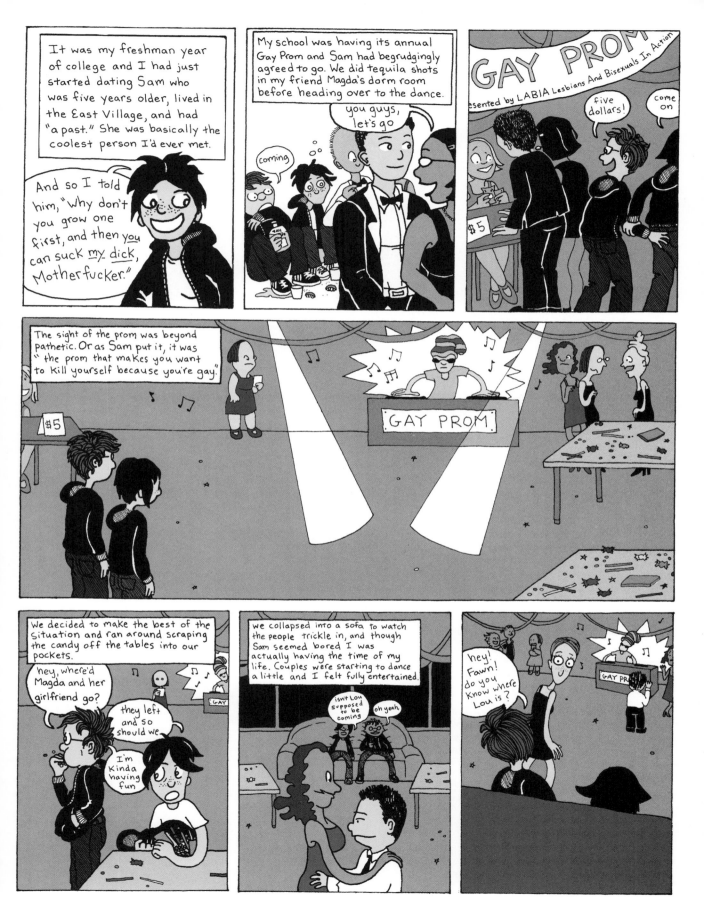

It was my freshman year of college and I had just started dating Sam who was five years older, lived in the East Village, and had "a past." She was basically the coolest person I'd ever met.

And so I told him, "Why don't you grow one first, and then you can suck my dick, Motherfucker."

My school was having its annual Gay Prom and Sam had begrudgingly agreed to go. We did tequila shots in my friend Magda's dorm room before heading over to the dance.

you guys, let's go

coming

GAY PROM

Presented by LABIA Lesbians And Bisexuals In Action

five dollars!

come on

$5

The sight of the prom was beyond pathetic. Or as Sam put it, it was "the prom that makes you want to kill yourself because you're gay."

$5

GAY PROM

We decided to make the best of the situation and ran around scraping the candy off the tables into our pockets.

hey, where'd Magda and her girlfriend go?

they left and so should we.

I'm kinda having fun

GAY

We collapsed into a sofa to watch the people trickle in, and though Sam seemed bored I was actually having the time of my life. Couples were starting to dance a little and I felt fully entertained.

isn't Lou supposed to be coming

oh yeah.

hey! Fawn! do you know where Lou is?

GAY PR

59

Lou's not coming! Jenny said something to her! They're my two best friends! I don't know what to do! She's not coming!
GAY PROM
we should call her
We followed Fawn to a pay phone where she called Lou (who was, by the way, my best friend, not Fawn's).
I've been crying in the bathroom for 25 minutes, I understand if you can't come, I can't handle this!
let's go downtown
NO! you can't leave! this is my fancy dance I organized!
can I talk to Lou?
I'm leaving
Lou? what happened!
"sh-she said, y-you're the most irritating FFUCKED-UP person I've ever met" huhhh huhh
well she sucks! we knew that, so who cares!?
NO, I like w-worshiped her, sh-she was so beautiful, she hates me
look, just come here, ok?
huhhh huhh, ok...
I found Sam looking aimless inside the dance where significantly more people had aggregated and were dancing. We shuffled around, bored, until Sam found somebody's lost wallet and the fun began.
come on! let's go look through it in the bathroom!
AY PROM
eight dollars
College ID, her name is Susan Marcus
Ohio State Drivers License
Metro card
anything else? Check all the flaps
uh, no, that's it. This $8 is too pathetic to steal
yeah... let's go find Susan Marcus!
yeah! let's find Susan Marcus
SUSAN MARCUS!
SUSAN MARCUS
SUSAN MARCUS?
SUSAN MARCUS!
No, but I know her
DON'T TELL ME! we'll find her!
uh, no
excuse me, Susan Marcus?
hey! there's Lou!

Lou! you came! fuck Jenny! fuck 'er!
yeah! fuck 'er
Lou's a little drunk
Lou! we're gonna get Jenny for you!
you're gonna get in a fight?
I have never been in a fight before!
Do it! I got your back!
WE'RE GONNA KICK HER ASS!
OK!
DON'T TOUCH JENNY, ARIEL! DON'T YOU TOUCH HER!
this is the boringest conversation, let's go find Susan Marcus
Don't touch her, Lou, don't let her touch her
After a few more unsuccessful tries we came upon a pudgy straight-haired girl in awkward fancy clothes.
yes, I'm Susan Marcus
prove it!
prove you're Susan Marcus!
I- I-
I can't 'cause,
'cause you have my wallet?
you're from Ohio!
we didn't steal your money!

There wasn't much to say after that, so we parted ways, and now, lacking the Susan Marcus search, Sam and I turned to the Jenny ordeal.
Lou! Where's Jenny! I forget what she looks like! We're gonna get her!
I don't know, I thought I saw her, she has blonde hair?
We circled the dance floor and though we couldn't find Jenny we did manage to round up some backup.
Bryah! you got our back, right!
yeah, I got your back
Katharine, when we start throwin' punches, you got our back?
well, I got your spiritual back, but
Susan Marcus, I KNOW you got our back
I got your back!
And finally, I spotted the familiar couple of Jenny and Margaret in an embraced dance and sucking face.
that's them! I'm nervous!
come on, you can do it!
what do I do?!
you say, "you're the most irritating person I've ever met," and then you punch her in the face
ok, I'm gonna do it
I got your back
tap tap
you're the most irritating person I've ever met
BAM
Don't-

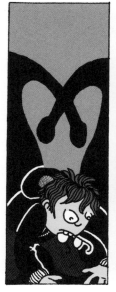
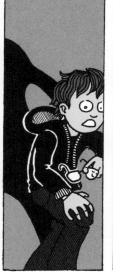
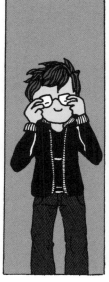
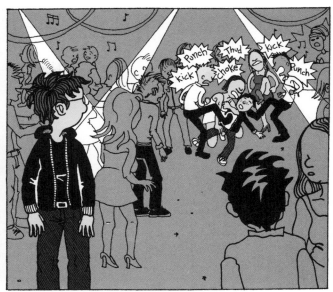

Punch
Thud
Kick
Kick
Choke
Punch

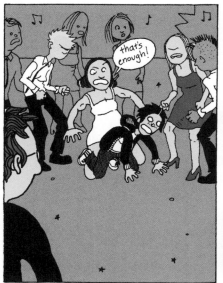

that's enough!

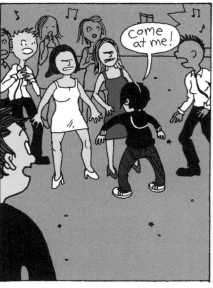

come at me!

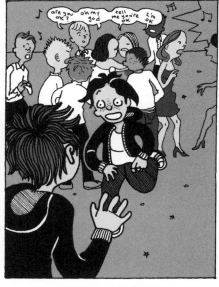

are you ok? oh my god tell me you're ok I'm ok

It appeared to be over. Sam and I slunk to the sidelines where I embraced Lou.

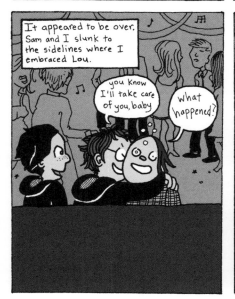

you know I'll take care of you, baby

What happened?

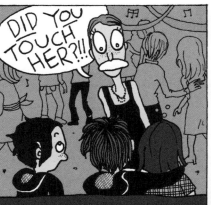

DID YOU TOUCH HER?!!

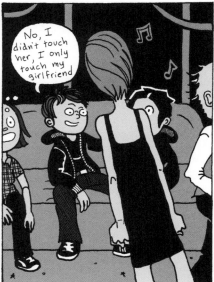

No, I didn't touch her, I only touch my girlfriend

do you wanna dance? let's have fun, will you dance with me?
uh no, I don't dance
DID YOU TOUCH HER!
No I didn't touch her
I didn't touch her, I punched her in the face
YOU'RE OUT!! GET OUT!!
fine
GAY PROM
Presented by LABIA Lesbians and Bisexuals in Action
Lou our friendship is over
excuse me
excuse me, I'm going to have to ask you to leave
GAY
that was fucked up! that was really fucked up
whatever
UNIVERSITY
over there, officer
you guys wanna tell me what happened at this uh- this party, you punched someone?
well, we were on the dance floor, and there was some shoving, and she was on the ground being kicked, you know how it happens

I'm the organizer of this event and I'm friends with all the parties involved and I know what happened
did you witness the fight?
Well no, but I saw preemptive, and I'm the organizer—
ah, that's ok, you can leave.
What are you even doing here, Sam? What are you? Somebody's girlfriend? Why are you even dating a college girl?
why are you a college girl?
The police continued to ask us how it started and suddenly, for some reason, lying seemed like death.
so why did you punch her?
she said something to my friend
and there was the shoving
I need to write a report so what's your answer?
She said something.
After that, they just let us go.
Back in my room, we changed into our pajamas.
I think they cracked a rib! It's like I can still feel it!
It was actually kinda hot...
We got into bed and Sam wanted to have sex.
come on
No...
I tried to fall asleep.
Why did I do that? What was I thinking? I'm a good, peaceful person! ...Aren't I?

It's Sam's fault.
Yeah, that's it, Sam made me do it...
It's not Sam's fault
Just stop thinking about it. It's over, OK? It's over.
It was just a dumb fight at the dumb gay prom. No one will remember, it's over. It's over...
It's over...
But it will never be over.
I'm sorry.

Home for the Holidays
2001 age 21

home for the holidays.
Beean
byan.
red T-shirt's in the house.
Haley isn't.
Hubbard's done gone crazy.
oh you!
mom!
showdown.
showdown?
and Shmally, from time to time.
who's there!
Zally and Ariel!
There was the skin doctor.
ACNE
so what's this about?
I have some moles
the breast doctor.
so what's going on?
I have some lumps
the Dalai Lama
and the physical therapist.
good.
tomorrow is the throat doctor.
I'm sorry to say, but you have both tuberculosis and cystic fibrosis.
Sam on the phone.
Sami's place!
Jonathan Louise got breast implants!
raspy polyps!
Sami's place.
I go by byan.
and danger in my dreams.

Wandering Hands

2003 age 23

1.

what the...
oh
it's just wandering hands

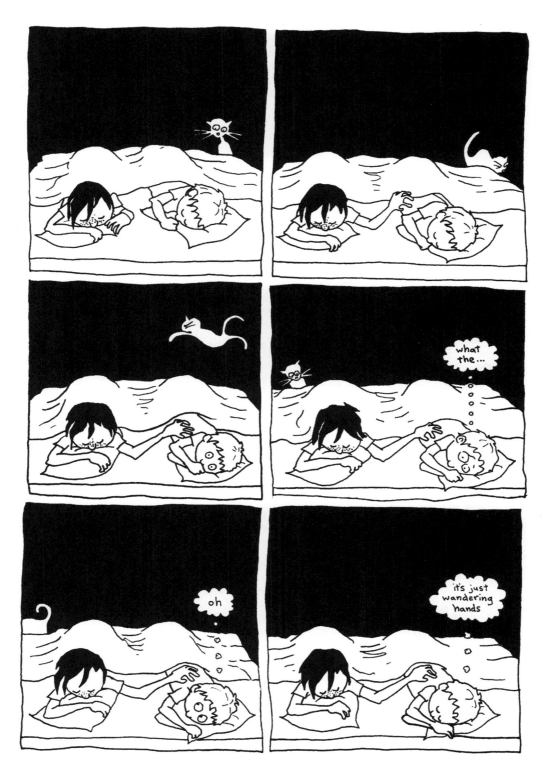

2.

wandering hands!
wandering hands!
heeheeheeh heeeheheee

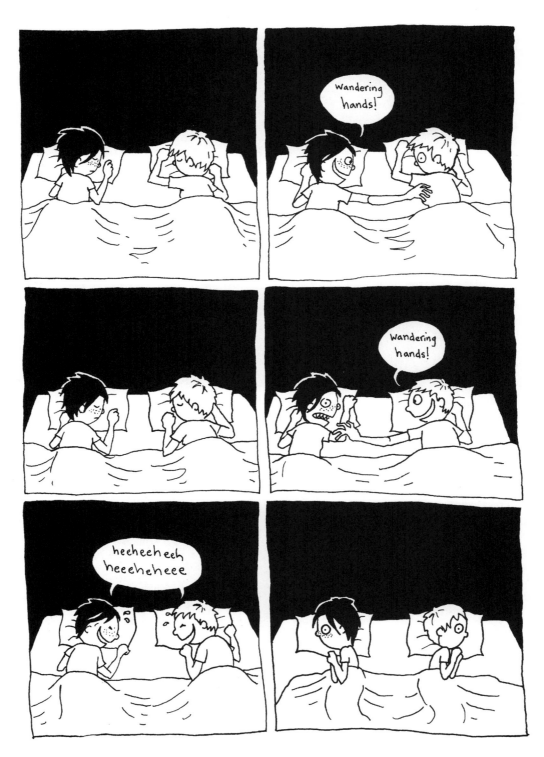

3.

hey, you can crash here if you want
thanks
wandering hands

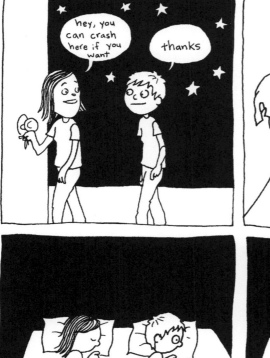

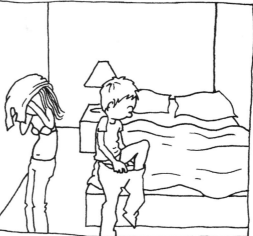

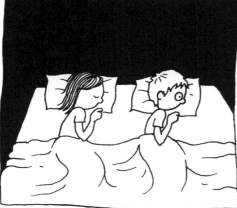

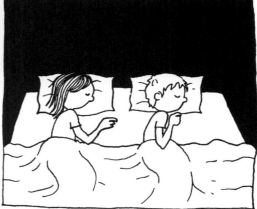

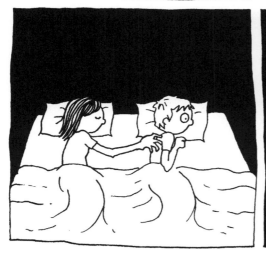

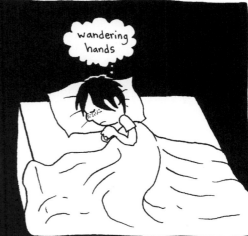

My Troubles with Glasses

2004 age 24

my troubles with
GLASSES
It all began one night in December of 2003, my first year after graduating college. I was working studiously at my desk when I casually took off my glasses to rub away some smudge with my shirt.
SNAP
It seemed almost inconceivable. These glasses were my trusty steadfasts. They'd been with me for years.
Five to be exact. I'd bought them my first year in New York after my others were crushed during a fit of passion.
CRUNCH
The buying of the new glasses back then had been relatively painless. I'd gone to LensCrafters and picked out the most similar looking black plastic pair. True, these ones had (mildly traumatizing) golden dots on the stems...
why?
...but after a week or so I forgot all about this slight imperfection and the glasses melded perfectly into a part of me.
I told myself it was time now to make that change again. It would be fun, I'd find a new pair, and maybe this time they wouldn't even have the annoying golden dots. As for right now, I'd just get by with superglue.

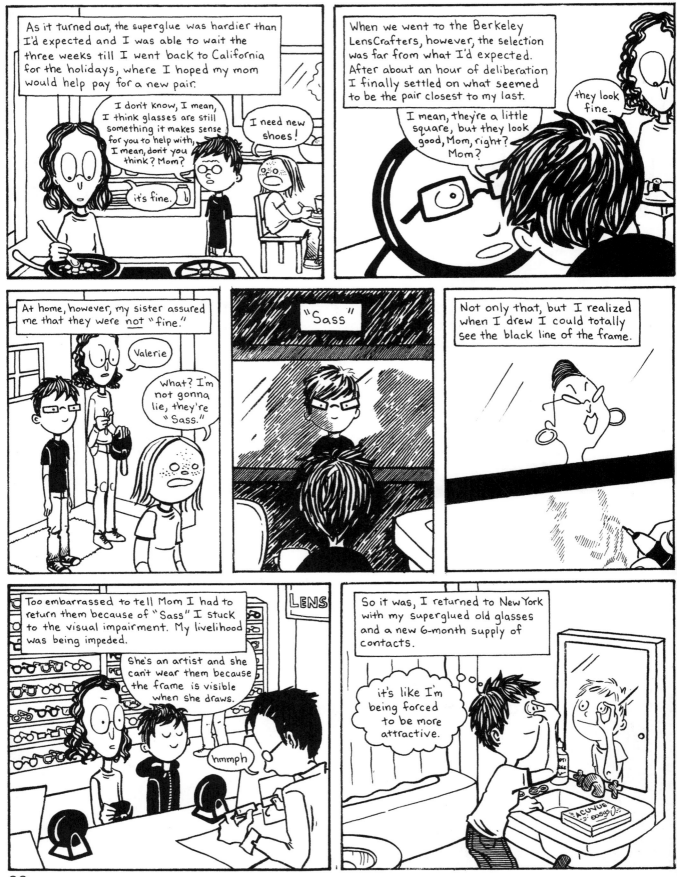

As it turned out, the superglue was hardier than I'd expected and I was able to wait the three weeks till I went back to California for the holidays, where I hoped my mom would help pay for a new pair.

I don't know, I mean, I think glasses are still something it makes sense for you to help with, I mean, don't you think? Mom?

it's fine.

I need new shoes!

When we went to the Berkeley LensCrafters, however, the selection was far from what I'd expected. After about an hour of deliberation I finally settled on what seemed to be the pair closest to my last.

I mean, they're a little square, but they look good, Mom, right? Mom?

they look fine.

At home, however, my sister assured me that they were not "fine."

Valerie

What? I'm not gonna lie, they're "Sass."

"Sass"

Not only that, but I realized when I drew I could totally see the black line of the frame.

Too embarrassed to tell Mom I had to return them because of "Sass" I stuck to the visual impairment. My livelihood was being impeded.

She's an artist and she can't wear them because the frame is visible when she draws.

hmmph

LENS

So it was, I returned to New York with my superglued old glasses and a new 6-month supply of contacts.

it's like I'm being forced to be more attractive.

ACUVUE

80

When I was younger I had just figured I would wear contacts and only contacts for the rest of my life. I was discovered to be nearsighted in 6th grade and glasses at this time were simply not an option.

popular
dating
fun
music
glasses.

Still, my parents wouldn't let me get contacts until I graduated 8th grade, so for the next two years I just went around blind.

The only time I did dare to wear my glasses was when I was at home watching TV, but even then they could work against me.

No! I'm watching that show.

No! I wanna watch my show!

heeheh heh

WHAT?!

you look so stupid standing there wearing your glasses.

Nothing made one more vulnerable than glasses.

As far as my sister was concerned, though, it didn't take my parents too long to diagnose her as well.

The day of my 8th grade graduation my parents gave me (and my sister – NOT FAIR) contacts. The world came into focus and I thought I'd never look back.

♪ LEAN ON ME ♫ WE ALL NEEEED SOMEBODY ♪

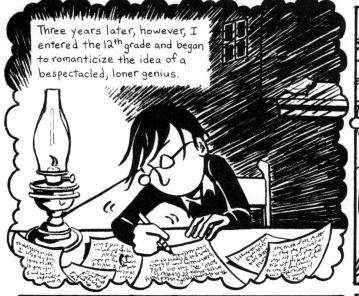

Three years later, however, I entered the 12th grade and began to romanticize the idea of a bespectacled, loner genius.

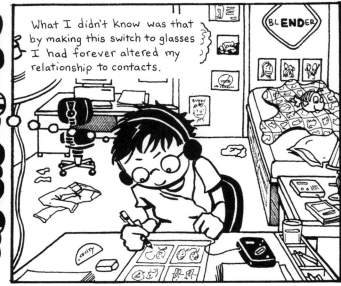

What I didn't know was that by making this switch to glasses I had forever altered my relationship to contacts.

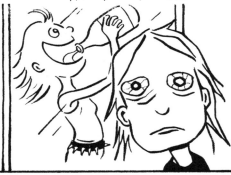

Three more years later, when I was bored of "genius" and thought I'd go back to the long-blonde-haired-16-hour-contacts days of my teens, something had changed. Just like I could no longer drink 3 forties, 6 shots of vodka, and wake up fine, so it was with contacts. Now, along with the hangovers, over 7 hours of contacts-wearing resulted in a bleary, sore, red-eyed mess.

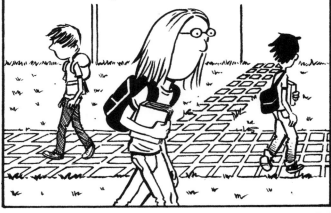

Despite my plans I ended up just wearing glasses most of the time and instead of reclaiming my Gwen Stefani teen look I spent most of college walking around like a glasses-wearing member of Hanson.

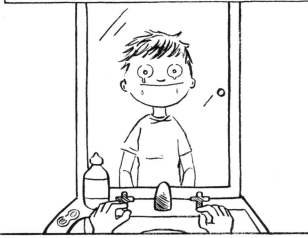

Now, with my glasses in fragile, superglued condition, I had no choice. I needed to spare my time with glasses and maximize on contacts.

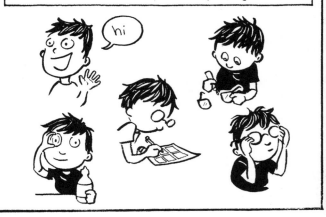

So, for the next 7 months I wore contacts outside, glasses inside, supergluing every two weeks as needed. Sometimes I thought about looking for a new pair of glasses, but the memory of "Sass" still haunted me – and I became accustomed to my contacts/superglue routine.

hi

Until one day, the superglue stopped working.
7:00
KRAZY
I tried reapplying and holding them together for 15 minutes. Didn't work. Reapplying and holding for 25 minutes. Didn't work. Reapplying and holding for the entire length of The Eminem Show album.
I'm a soldier
7:57
KRAZY
Still didn't work.
Finally, I tried hacking away at all the dried old superglue with an exacto knife and then reapplying.
No good.
8:30
KRAZY
I was without glasses.
11:58
OPTI FREE
The day after my glasses broke for good I was on a bus driving up to rural Maine to spend the week helping my mom and sister take care of my grandmother at her summer house.
I decided I would just have to wear contacts for most of the time and go blind when my eyes were tired. Since I would only be around family in the woods it shouldn't be a problem.
There was, in fact, something I really liked about being extremely nearsighted. It was like I could exist in two separate universes.
the city has sunk underwater
During my blind days in junior high I used to imagine that I was developing my other senses at an accelerated rate.
Get her to the ER!
why are you facing over there?
It is easier for me to understand this way.
My vision was 10 times worse now than it had been back then and I imagined myself in Maine, re-sharpening my old skills.
Hark! A loon!
really?
I don't hear it!

When I arrived in Maine, however, all romantic ideas about being blind were forgotten and replaced by a sudden, desperate need to be mothered and taken care of.
Ariel!
Mom! I need you to fix my glasses!
That night, my mom spent three hours coming up with some elaborate thread-cardboard-superglue method of holding together the glasses.
I, meanwhile, did impressions of my roommate's restless cat, Mumford, for my sister.
Mumford can't settle!
WOOLF
Hah! I knew I could do it! How do they work?!
um, they don't really stay on my face... sorry...
I am going to bed, so you will need to please not talk so loud.
I figured I would just go back to the being blind plan, but the next morning my mom was all business about going to buy me new glasses. It felt wrong, wrong, this was not how I was supposed to buy new ones, it was only a week, I could wait and get them in New York, but Mom was in control, Mom was taking care...
the nearest glasses store is an hour and a half away, we'll be back around 4:30.
So I did it.
If the LensCrafters in Berkeley was bad, I couldn't begin to explain this tiny shop tucked away in a woodland crevice of rural Maine. Plastic frames of any kind were not even an option here. Yet despite the limited selection it still took me over an hour to settle on a thin, round, wire frame Brooks Brothers pair.
We do all the work right here at the shop, but there's only two of us. We should have them by tomorrow.
All right
WELCOME
I decided that not being able to choose another black plastic pair was a sign. Wire frames were the new me! Away with this indie rock-pseudo-film director bullshit. These were respectable and practical, just glasses, simply glasses.
you know, I feel really good about these new glasses.
I was just thinking the same thing.

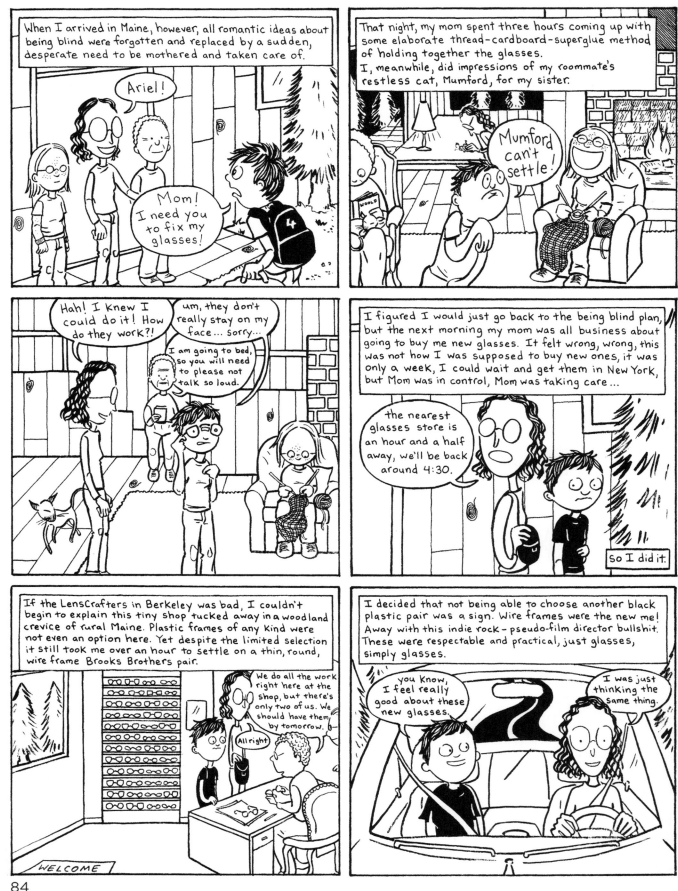

But about an hour after we got home, I started to have a little problem.
why can't I seem to stop thinking about those glasses
After dinner, I decided to send my best friend Sam a lighthearted text message just to get some reassurance.
I got some nerdy wire frames.
DISGRACE
MAGIC MOUNTAIN
oh my god you're kidding. You CANNOT wear wire frames
WHAT HAD I DONE
As I got into bed everything was a blur of glasses. What had I been thinking? Why didn't I just wait? There was nothing I could do now, there was nothing I could do, I would just have to deal, I was nerd now, No! NO! What was I thinking, they were wrong! WRONG! Why couldn't I go back? I couldn't go back, these were my glasses, this was my future, just deal, don't think about it, forget about it, don't think about it.
BREASTS

I woke up in the morning with glasses glued to the inside of my brain.
In a last, desperate attempt, I sent Sam another text.
Look. I just really need your support with these glasses. OK?
Return them
I sat down to breakfast deeply, horridly ashamed.
So we're going into Ellsworth to pick up Ariel's glasses and we'll get something for dinner in Bar Harbor on the way back.
I don't want to pick up theglasses.
JULY
no one heard me.
JULY
JULY
I think I need to return the glasses.
WHAT!
Ariel! Don't be ridiculous. This whole thing with the glasses has been ridiculous!
Y- you don't understand! It's not that easy! It's the only thing I can think about.
I understand.
Well, I'm sorry. I didn't realize you were that crazy.
Well, I am.

So I returned the glasses.
I-I just decided I don't want them.
but the glass is already cut! We normally don't have a return policy like this - I mean, I suppose we can refund you - but we'd be making an exception.
th-thank you
I'm sorry, Mom, I'm so sorry.
It's OK. I just don't think I'll be going with you to buy any more glasses.
C'mon, Ariel! Let's go out in the boat.
Free of the glasses the world had never looked so glorious.

When I got back to New York I decided this time I was absolutely going to do things right. I arranged a date in which the whole day was free for me and Sam to go to the largest LensCrafters in the city. I even arrived two hours before she was meeting me so that I could make preliminary judgments.
LENSCRAFTERS
PRADA
$ 50 OFF EYEGLASSES W/ PURCHASE
OAKLEY
PRESCRIPTION COLLECTION
20% OFF LENSES WITH FRAME PRESCRIPT LIMITED TIME OFFER
When Sam arrived we stayed for another three hours.
OK, so I was thinking these are the best.
No.
The guy here recommended these...
No.
teal
Are you sure I shouldn't do wire frames?
Yes.
I look like a genius, don't I?! These make me look like a genius!
Do they make me look like a genius?
No.
Too Williamsburg
Too Dyke Rock
Too Lauryn Siegel

Finally, Sam convinced me that the best bet was a pair of tan, slightly iridescent Armani frames.
You're sure they're not too iridescent?
It's barely noticeable. Trust me. Those are the best.
these really do make me look like a genius. Should I just buy them with clear glass?
That will be $290. Credit or debit?
The decision was made. I should have felt free, liberated...
ENSC
FREE 30-DAY TRIAL
But instead, when I went back the next day to pick up the finished glasses, the truth was undeniably locked.
So, uh... what color would you say these glasses are?
I had just purchased:
purple, shimmery, sparkling, iridescent
glasses.
That night I went to see the movie "A Home at the End of the World" with my friends Magda and Lou. I was unable to think of anything other than the characters' glasses.
Oh, shit, I gotta go-
yeah, yeah, I got it
Hmm, so, as a teenager he wore the seventies, large-line-across-the-top gold wire frames, which went great with the long hair. Now he's wearing round, black... wire or plastic? I think I detect nose pads-wire. They're sort of owlish, yet they complicate the face just right. Now his boss has orange plastic frames...
How perfect they were for each of them-and how unbelievably wrong mine were for me.

The next day, all I did was imagine myself in different scenarios wearing my purple, shimmery, iridescent glasses.
THUMP THUMP
at a party
going to the deli
pepper turkey with American cheese on a roll.
at a No Doubt concert in 10th grade
a fire
MY Baby!
I wonder if this light brings out the iridescence in my glasses
teaching
I can't concentrate on a word she's saying, all I can think about are those sparkly glasses
on a plane
I wonder why a dykish girl like that would wear iridescent glasses?
ZZZZ
watching TV with Sam
meet me at Bada Bing
meeting with an Agent
WIIIAM MORR
I would like to represent her, but I mean, those glasses... does she really know what she's doing?
Spending the night at my ex-girlfriend Haley's house
I can't believe I just got fucked by someone who wears iridescent glasses

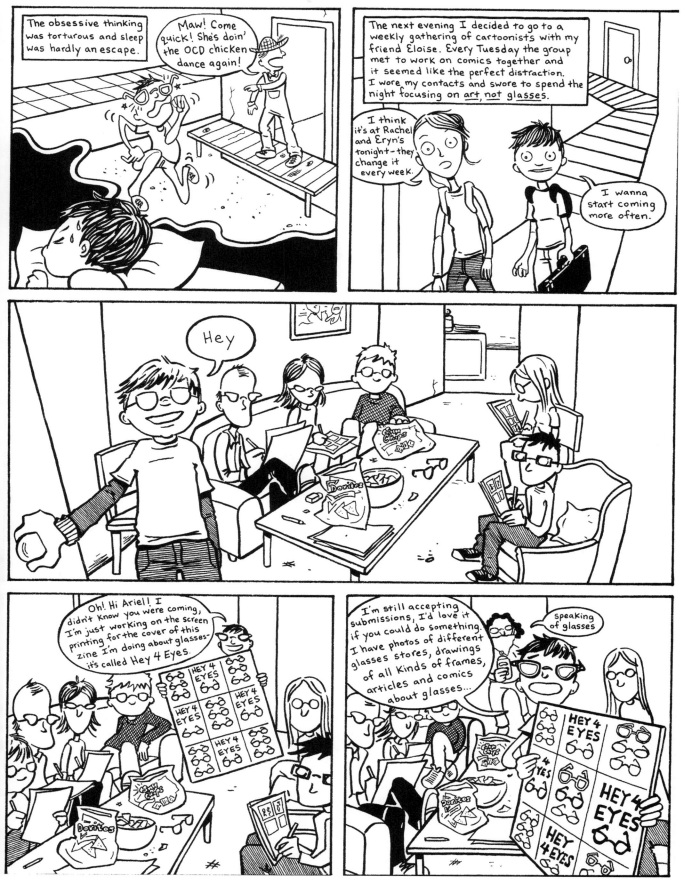

The obsessive thinking was torturous and sleep was hardly an escape.

Maw! Come quick! She's doin' the OCD chicken dance again!

The next evening I decided to go to a weekly gathering of cartoonists with my friend Eloise. Every Tuesday the group met to work on comics together and it seemed like the perfect distraction. I wore my contacts and swore to spend the night focusing on art, not glasses.

I think it's at Rachel and Eryn's tonight — they change it every week.

I wanna start coming more often.

Hey

Oh! Hi Ariel! I didn't know you were coming, I'm just working on the screen printing for the cover of this zine I'm doing about glasses — it's called Hey 4 Eyes.

HEY 4 EYES
HEY 4 EYES
HEY 4 EYES

I'm still accepting submissions, I'd love it if you could do something. I have photos of different glasses stores, drawings of all kinds of frames, articles and comics about glasses...

speaking of glasses

HEY 4 EYES
4 EYES
HEY 4 EYES

can I just tell you, I tried to buy these new glasses, but my PD is off, that's pupillary distance, how far apart your pupils are from each other,
HEY 4 EYES
it corresponds with the optical center of the lens, the optical center should line up with your pupils. But my PD is smaller than normal, it's 55, and even things a millimeter off make things look warped and give me an eyeache,
So I went to LensCrafters, and I went to Cohen Optical, but they all thought I was crazy, they don't believe me about my PD, but I know it's true
I, um, I actually think I have to go.
Safe at home, alone with my glasses, I tried to find a way to just finally accept them. As I stared at their color in the light it started to come to me... I told myself that these were my magical glasses. That's why they were sparkly – because in fact they were magic and gave me secret powers. Yes! For the rest of my life, whenever I write or draw, I must always be wearing my magical glasses!!!
Clearly, I needed to return the glasses.

After I returned the iridescents I decided that this time what I needed to do was in every way possible recreate that blissful, simple experience of buying my 2nd pair of black glasses 6 years ago. So, at what seemed like the same hour of the day I went alone to the same small LensCrafters on the Upper East Side...

None of this ever happened. I've just broken my glasses and I'm simply going to buy another pair.

THE SALE 50% LENSES

It only took about 5 minutes of being inside to be hit with an attack of explosive diarrhea.

RESTROOM

FLUSH

But once that was over, things seemed to go pretty smoothly. After scanning the entire collection it was clear that there weren't any black glasses even remotely close to my old ones. For some inexplicable reason, they just didn't seem to be made anymore. But this was fine, and when my eyes fell on a pair of silver wire frames with modest winged tips something told me — these are the ones.

it's as if they've always belonged there.

I was so confident, in fact, that when the glasses clerk tried to persuade me they weren't right, I just chuckled nonchalantly.

What? you don't like my glasses?

they just seem a little... big... maybe.

No. These are the ones. Thanks.

I picked the finished glasses up an hour later...

and then returned them after 20 minutes because I was convinced the lenses had been inserted unevenly.

You see how you can see the edge of it coming out in front on this side, but not on this side?

They told me that in order to fix it they would have to replace the glasses with new lenses, which meant ordering them from another store, which meant they wouldn't be ready until tomorrow.
So I went home to wait.

these are the ones
these are the ones

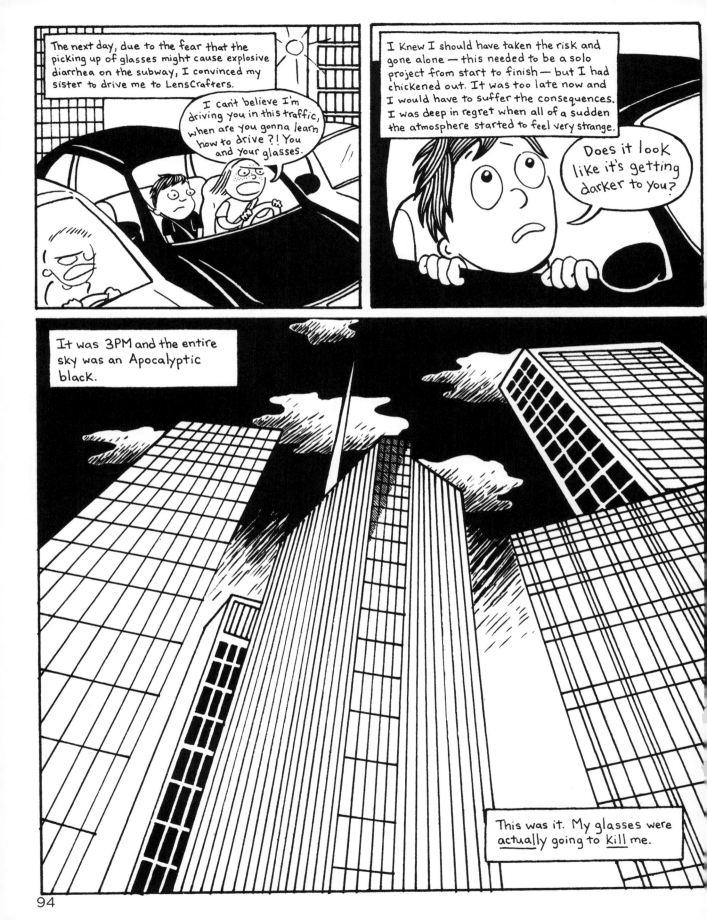

The next day, due to the fear that the picking up of glasses might cause explosive diarrhea on the subway, I convinced my sister to drive me to LensCrafters.

I can't believe I'm driving you in this traffic, when are you gonna learn how to drive?! You and your glasses.

I knew I should have taken the risk and gone alone — this needed to be a solo project from start to finish — but I had chickened out. It was too late now and I would have to suffer the consequences. I was deep in regret when all of a sudden the atmosphere started to feel very strange.

Does it look like it's getting darker to you?

It was 3PM and the entire sky was an Apocalyptic black.

This was it. My glasses were actually going to kill me.

CRASH
BOOM
HONK
HONK
HONK

My sister pulled the car over to a curb. We waited for about ten minutes, but when it didn't seem to be getting any better I decided to brave it and ran out, plowing through the torrents, making my way to LensCrafters.
When I returned, wearing the glasses, the rain had weakened to a slight drizzle.

OK. When I saw you across the street my first thought was "Sass," but... up close... they're fine.
shut

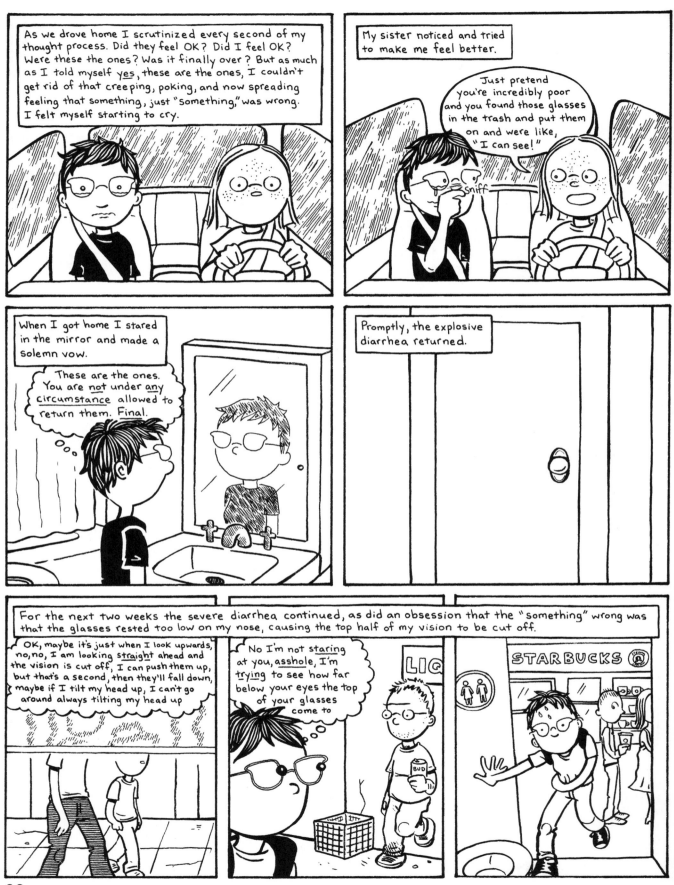

As we drove home I scrutinized every second of my thought process. Did they feel OK? Did I feel OK? Were these the ones? Was it finally over? But as much as I told myself yes, these are the ones, I couldn't get rid of that creeping, poking, and now spreading feeling that something, just "something," was wrong. I felt myself starting to cry.

My sister noticed and tried to make me feel better.

Just pretend you're incredibly poor and you found those glasses in the trash and put them on and were like, "I can see!"

Sniff

When I got home I stared in the mirror and made a solemn vow.

These are the ones. You are not under any circumstance allowed to return them. Final.

Promptly, the explosive diarrhea returned.

For the next two weeks the severe diarrhea continued, as did an obsession that the "something" wrong was that the glasses rested too low on my nose, causing the top half of my vision to be cut off.

OK, maybe it's just when I look upwards, no, no, I am looking straight ahead and the vision is cut off, I can push them up, but that's a second, then they'll fall down, maybe if I tilt my head up, I can't go around always tilting my head up

No I'm not staring at you, asshole, I'm trying to see how far below your eyes the top of your glasses come to

LIQ

BUD

STARBUCKS

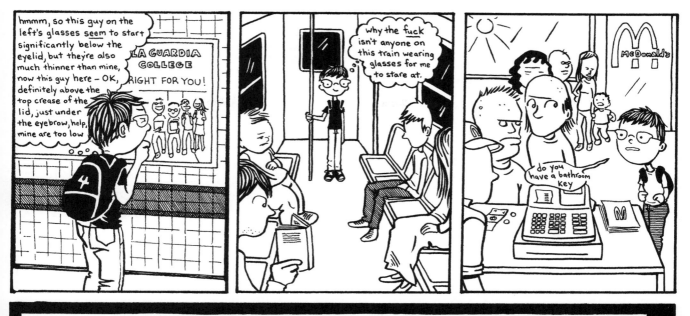

Panel 1 (thought): hmmm, so this guy on the left's glasses seem to start significantly below the eyelid, but they're also much thinner than mine, now this guy here – OK, definitely above the top crease of the lid, just under the eyebrow, help, mine are too low

LA GUARDIA COLLEGE
RIGHT FOR YOU!

Panel 2 (thought): why the fuck isn't anyone on this train wearing glasses for me to stare at.

Panel 3: McDonald's
do you have a bathroom key

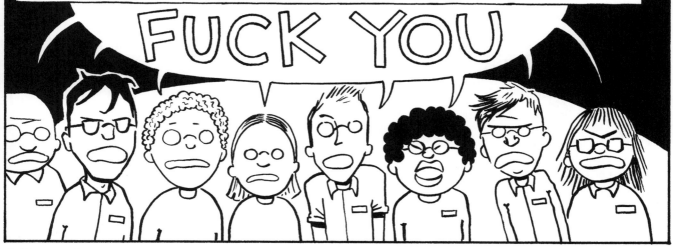

And whenever my mind betrayed itself enough to entertain that slight possibility... I could ... return them ... the same waking nightmare appeared.

FUCK YOU

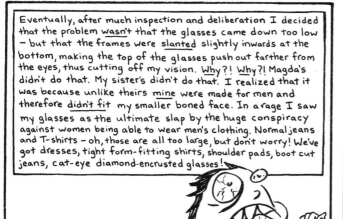

Eventually, after much inspection and deliberation I decided that the problem wasn't that the glasses came down too low – but that the frames were slanted slightly inwards at the bottom, making the top of the glasses push out farther from the eyes, thus cutting off my vision. Why?! Why?! Magda's didn't do that. My sister's didn't do that. I realized that it was because unlike theirs mine were made for men and therefore didn't fit my smaller boned face. In a rage I saw my glasses as the ultimate slap by the huge conspiracy against women being able to wear men's clothing. Normal jeans and T-shirts – oh, those are all too large, but don't worry! We've got dresses, tight form-fitting shirts, shoulder pads, boot cut jeans, cat-eye diamond-encrusted glasses!

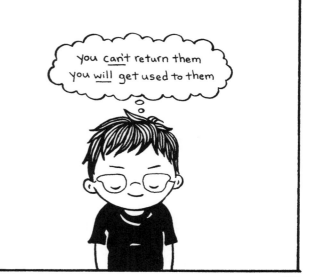

(thought): you can't return them you will get used to them

97

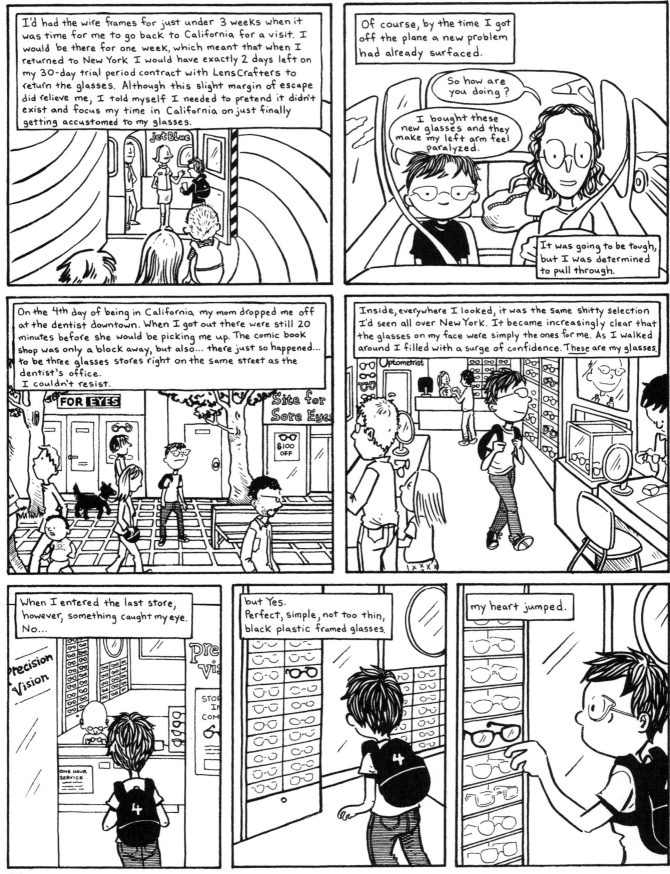

I'd had the wire frames for just under 3 weeks when it was time for me to go back to California for a visit. I would be there for one week, which meant that when I returned to New York I would have exactly 2 days left on my 30-day trial period contract with LensCrafters to return the glasses. Although this slight margin of escape did relieve me, I told myself I needed to pretend it didn't exist and focus my time in California on just finally getting accustomed to my glasses.

Of course, by the time I got off the plane a new problem had already surfaced.

So how are you doing?

I bought these new glasses and they make my left arm feel paralyzed.

It was going to be tough, but I was determined to pull through.

On the 4th day of being in California my mom dropped me off at the dentist downtown. When I got out there were still 20 minutes before she would be picking me up. The comic book shop was only a block away, but also... there just so happened... to be three glasses stores right on the same street as the dentist's office.
I couldn't resist.

FOR EYES
Site for Sore Eyes
$100 OFF

Inside, everywhere I looked, it was the same shitty selection I'd seen all over New York. It became increasingly clear that the glasses on my face were simply the ones for me. As I walked around I filled with a surge of confidence. These are my glasses.

Optometrist

When I entered the last store, however, something caught my eye. No...

Precision Vision

ONE HOUR SERVICE

but Yes.
Perfect, simple, not too thin, black plastic framed glasses.

my heart jumped.

No, no, I couldn't get sucked back in, the wire frames were my glasses.
the wire frames were the ones, I made a pact.
this never happened, this never happened.
precision Vision
How are your teeth?
Fine.
That night, I talked on the phone with Sam.
but they're like the perfect black ones I've been searching for.
You don't want black plastic – they're played out. I like your wire frames. I was getting used to looking at you in them.
OK, but can we just go over the plus and minuses of the black ones? If I buy them I'll still have two days to return the wire frames to LensCrafters.
You cannot go back to LensCrafters! They're going to have a warning sign up on their wall about you. Besides, if you buy the black ones you'll just find another problem with them.
You're right. I won't buy them. I'll just get used to the wire frames.
We hung up. My mom was over at her boyfriend's and I was alone. The house was creepy and still.
I wandered into my mom's bedroom and found an old photo album and started flipping through it. All I saw were the glasses.

The clear orange/brown '70s glasses my mom wore when I was a baby.
The thick-band-across-the-top black plastics my grandpa wore. Old men could get away with anything.
Uninteresting
My uncle with red/brow plastics and my dad wit those same wire frame interesting juxtapositio
The thin, perfectly shaped wire frames my dad wore. Absolutely perfect.
The reddish, large '70s glasses my aunt wore. Why wasn't big in style now? It would make things so much easier.
About halfway through the album I landed on a picture of me around age 13, wearing my very first original wire frames.
Sorenson's 1993
I never knew that any evidence of those glasses even existed. I stared at the photo in amazement, scrutinizing it, as if it were a crime-breaking clue.
I looked so casual, unconcerned. Playing Life and wearing glasses.
Where were those glasses now? What had happened to them? Were they in the bottom of some box? Crushed, thrown out?
Their physical matter was out there... somewhere in the world.

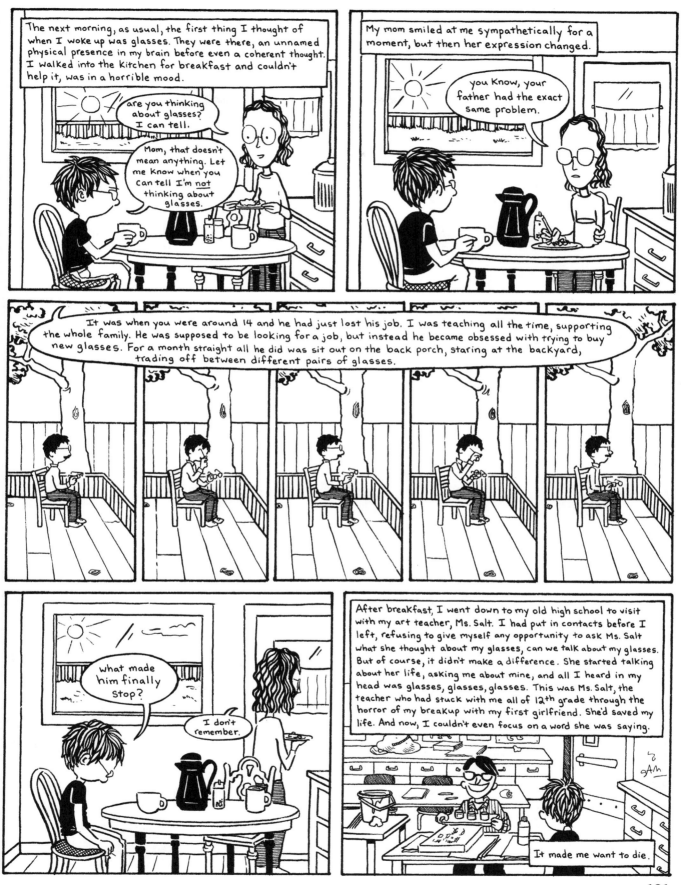

The next morning, as usual, the first thing I thought of when I woke up was glasses. They were there, an unnamed physical presence in my brain before even a coherent thought. I walked into the kitchen for breakfast and couldn't help it, was in a horrible mood.

are you thinking about glasses? I can tell.

Mom, that doesn't mean anything. Let me know when you can tell I'm not thinking about glasses.

My mom smiled at me sympathetically for a moment, but then her expression changed.

you know, your father had the exact same problem.

It was when you were around 14 and he had just lost his job. I was teaching all the time, supporting the whole family. He was supposed to be looking for a job, but instead he became obsessed with trying to buy new glasses. For a month straight all he did was sit out on the back porch, staring at the backyard, trading off between different pairs of glasses.

What made him finally stop?

I don't remember.

After breakfast, I went down to my old high school to visit with my art teacher, Ms. Salt. I had put in contacts before I left, refusing to give myself any opportunity to ask Ms. Salt what she thought about my glasses, can we talk about my glasses. But of course, it didn't make a difference. She started talking about her life, asking me about mine, and all I heard in my head was glasses, glasses, glasses. This was Ms. Salt, the teacher who had stuck with me all of 12th grade through the horror of my breakup with my first girlfriend. She'd saved my life. And now, I couldn't even focus on a word she was saying.

It made me want to die.

101

I'm, uh, I just have to run down to the glasses store really quick. I'm getting these new glasses.
OK! I love glasses!
I got outside and I started running
and I ran like my life depended on it.
Faster and faster as if with just enough speed
I could manage to outrun my own brain.
I got to the glasses store and picked up the perfect black plastic framed glasses. I tried them on and then, my heart racing, brought them to the store owner to buy.
I'm leaving town, so I would need to get them by tomorrow.
that's fine.
With a trembling hand I signed the non-refundable credit card bill.
Precision Vision
Two days later, back in New York, I put on large incognito sunglasses and returned the wire frames to LensCrafters.
LENSCRA
You're sure you don't want to exchange for another pair?
NO.

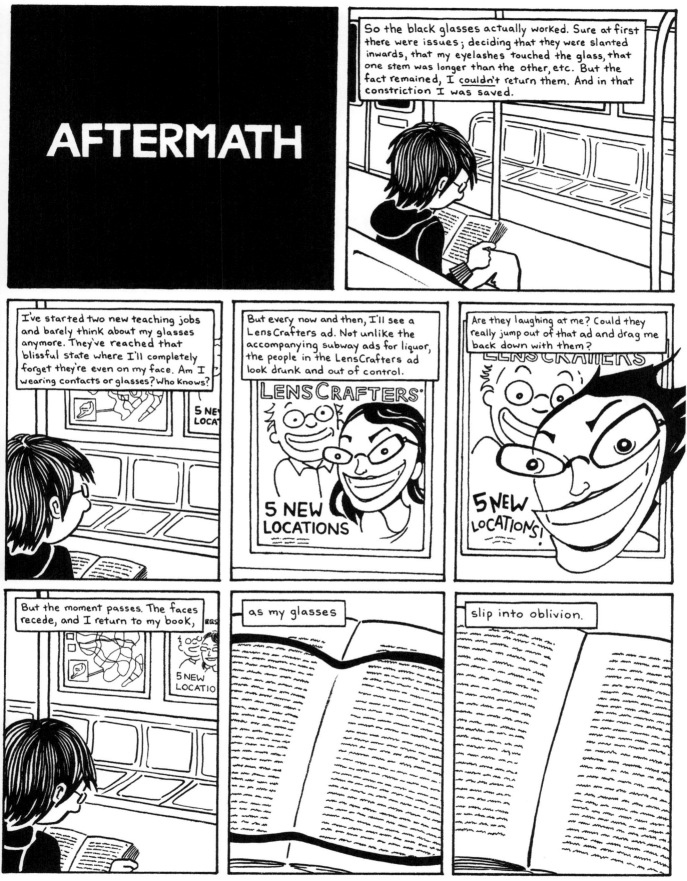

AFTERMATH

So the black glasses actually worked. Sure at first there were issues; deciding that they were slanted inwards, that my eyelashes touched the glass, that one stem was longer than the other, etc. But the fact remained, I couldn't return them. And in that constriction I was saved.

I've started two new teaching jobs and barely think about my glasses anymore. They've reached that blissful state where I'll completely forget they're even on my face. Am I wearing contacts or glasses? Who knows?

But every now and then, I'll see a LensCrafters ad. Not unlike the accompanying subway ads for liquor, the people in the LensCrafters ad look drunk and out of control.

LENSCRAFTERS
5 NEW LOCATIONS

Are they laughing at me? Could they really jump out of that ad and drag me back down with them?

LENSCRAFTERS
5 NEW LOCATIONS!

But the moment passes. The faces recede, and I return to my book,

as my glasses

slip into oblivion.

Kids Korner

2004 age 24

Kids Korner
I need a job I need a job I need a job I need a job I need a job I need a job I need a job
Craigslist Jobs NYC
Teaching
Latin Tutor
Full Time Administra
Math Tutor needed
CALC SAT tutor
Football coach
Budget $ rent utilities
Yes! Could this be it?! Part time art teacher needed for After School program! Middle School 86 in Harlem. Please send resumé. It's perfect!!
Craigslist Jobs NYC
Art Teacher Needed
M.S. 86
Part Time
Middle School
Painting
Drawing
Budget $ rent utilities
Tell me a little about your background in teaching.
Well I just graduated from college where I did America Reads and I also taught art at a YMCA summer camp in Berkeley. I can do painting, drawing, cartooning. I also like to teach drama.
That sounds great. Welcome!
great!
AFTER SCHO
M.S. 86
Ju-u-u-ust out of curiosity... What?! After School program art teacher needed $15 an hour?! That's $6 more than I'd be making at M.S. 86!!
Craigslist Jobs NYC
Art Teacher Needed
M.S. 137
Part Time
Middle School
$15/hr
Send resumé
Hi, Ms. Mendez? It's Ariel. I just wanted to let you know I actually have another potential offer so I won't be able to accept the position at this time.
THE BRAI
M.S. 137
guess all the kids have gone home. Feels kind of ominous around here.

this is the room they told me to go for the interview, but I've been waiting here 20 minutes...
Rm 17
Protocol requires I ask you the following set of questions have you or have you not ever been convicted of a felony please describe what you consider to be your greatest weakness what form of classroom management would you use if one of your students is being disruptive to the rest of the class please describe in specific detail what is your date of birth.
um, I, that is—
We will file this information and put it into our system, we will get back to you in 3 to 5 months we are not actually hiring right now.
M.S. 137
M-Ms. Mendez? It's Ariel! Is there any chance the position is still open?
JANUARY
We're just doing some mural painting, come join us!
Nooo!!! that's my part!
SCHOOL
S. 86
FASHION
ART
SPORTS
RESPECT
TRUTH
You look like a boy!
You look like a boy!
To be Continued...!

Kids Korner
starring...
Ms. A
age 24
OK, we can do portraits today—
YAYY!!!! I love portraits!!
But remember, NO drawing people ugly on purpose.
STAFF
Crayola
Ms. Thomas
age 25
I'm doing fashion for anyone who wants to follow.
YAYYY!!! Fashion! I'm doing fashion! I hate portraits anyway.
You alone in here, Ms. A?
Roxanne
age 11
Anyone that got anything to say to Natalia got to say it to me first.
Natalia
age 11
Yesterday, all I thought about was peace.
Shantey
age 12
I never in my life hit you with my belt in the lunchroom!
Ellen
age 11
Ms. A, you gothic? I wish I could be gothic but my mom won't let me wear make-up.
You know anyone gothic?
plus Nevin, Mia, Vanessa, Jace, Keisha, Serena, Anthony, Lanelle, Chloe, Ayana
and...
Ms. Mendez
age 29
OK, Natalia and Shantey, I want you each to tell me your side of the story and what you think happened. Does that sound fair?
Yes
OK, Shantey, you can start.
Not Fair!!
fair!

Kids Korner
OK, we're doing portraits. Now remember, look carefully at the person across from you and draw what you really see. Not what you think you see. Include every detail you can.
STAFF
This school is crazy. They think KG is the scariest projects, but—
When did Tyra Banks ever think about anyone in the world except herself.
Shantey, you need to be drawing Roxanne.
LL Cool J is almost a part of my family. He married my uncle's wife.
Ashanti is part of my family. She's my friend's cousin. Lil' Kim too. She's not my family, but she's like family to me. That's my god brother's aunt. 'Cause my god brother's sister married her aunt.
Shantey
Fabolous used to play dice with my father before he was rich.
Fabolous my cousin. I'm gonna tell the truth. I'm not trying to prove anything and I don't know his real name but Fabolous my cousin.
Somebody in my family used to be a famous basketball player.
Somebody in my family hit the lotto and never came back.
NAT

KIDS KORNER
OK, this is the next skit we're going to do: "A girl tells her parents she like another girl so they throw her out of the house."
STAFF
SKIT IDEAS
Who wrote THAT one?!
I did!
You get out this house it's a blasphemy!
You heard your mother it's a blasphemy!
You come near me I'll slap the hell out of you!
You can't tell her what to do, we're gonna live a happy life together!
TAFF
I'm just riding by on a bicycle
Ms. A, you got a girlfriend?
No.
AFF
You got a boyfriend?
No.
AFF
Ms. A, you lonely?
No.
AFF
Yes
AFF

Kids Korner
So Ariel, the school has decided to implement a girls sexual education program as part of After School and I'd like to talk to you about instructing it.
It's called "Girls Club" and it's very important, related to government mandate, that you stick to the messages and exercises in their official workbook.
ABSTINENCE IS THE WAY
OK, so the reason all the girls are in a room together is because this is "Girls Club," we'll be meeting once a week and talking about things related to dating, sex, and changes in the body.
Oooh you gonna get busted!
GIRLS CLUB
OK, so the first exercise we have here is a "dating scenario." Jacob and Susan are going out on a date. Jacob offers to pick Susan up in his car. Susan is not ready to engage in sexual activity so they decide to take the bus instead.
What are some other things Susan could have done besides taking the bus? Anyone?
GIRLS CLUB
Uh, anyone?
I hate Girls Club.
Girls Club is the worst thing that's ever happened to me in my entire life.

Uh, ok, how about this, we'll take this box and this will be the anonymous question box where you can ask any question that will be answered next "Girls Club."
Pencils
GIRLS
OFFICIAL
I'm writing two, Ms. A, are we allowed to write two?!
I'm writing three!
Mine is long.
I need a pen! I need a pen!
move, Ellen!
Pencils
STAFF
GIRLS CLUB
Pencils
If a woman have a penis and have sex with a guy can she stick it in his Butt if she want to.
GIRLS CLUB
pencils
How do a girl change that she is called a slut because she is sexual active?
does fagget mean?
what does queer mean?
Can a woman have like 10 to 15 hands inside her vagina?
What is a dildo and why do they call it that
C N SHANTY GET P EGNENT if a GIRL ellen stick HER ONGUE IN HER COOCH?
When a boy stick it in the back are you still a VergeAN
scoot
GIRLS CLUB
pencils
THUNK
pencils

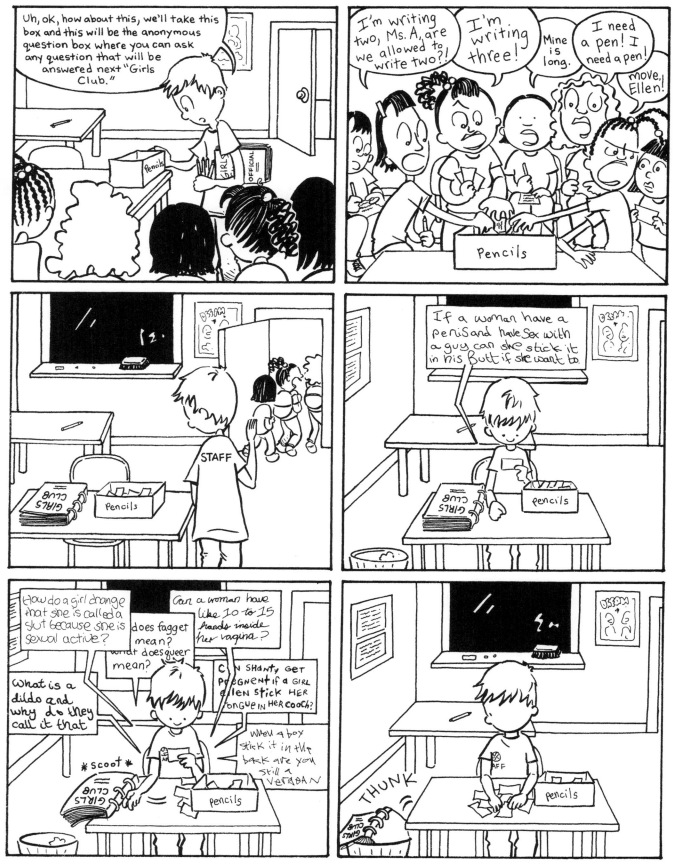

KIDS · KORNER
OK guys, today I want you to paint two pictures, one of your own personal heaven and one of your own personal hell.
I can't do that
I can't do that either
it's against my religion
STAFF
That's OK, it doesn't have to be religious, it can be what you see as paradise on earth or the worst place to live on earth.
What kind of religion are you, can't paint heaven or hell?
We're Jehovah's Witness
Y'all motherfuckers is oppressed.
STAFF
2x+3y= 7
Nothing wrong with Jehovah's Witness
My aunt is Jehovah's Witness and, yeah, I'm saying something's wrong with y'all. All she does is sit there. Now my mother, she's up and praying to Jesus.
You're supposed to let God go through you! Feel him through you! That's why people act like this! 'Cause God is going through their body!
STAFF
You felt God right then? Felt him going through you?
Natalia, you can have a discussion, but you need to take a seat and keep working on your painting.
OK, now who can explain to me in clear words the difference between these religions.
We don't go to heaven or hell, we're resurrected. I'm living forever.
Don't talk to me, Shantey, I'm not feeling it. Remember, Roxanne Bard said it from her own lips at M.S. 86 on February 23, 2004, you're going to heaven or hell. Resurrection my ass.
I'm living forever.
STAFF
You guys, you need to accept that people have different beliefs. You can't insult—

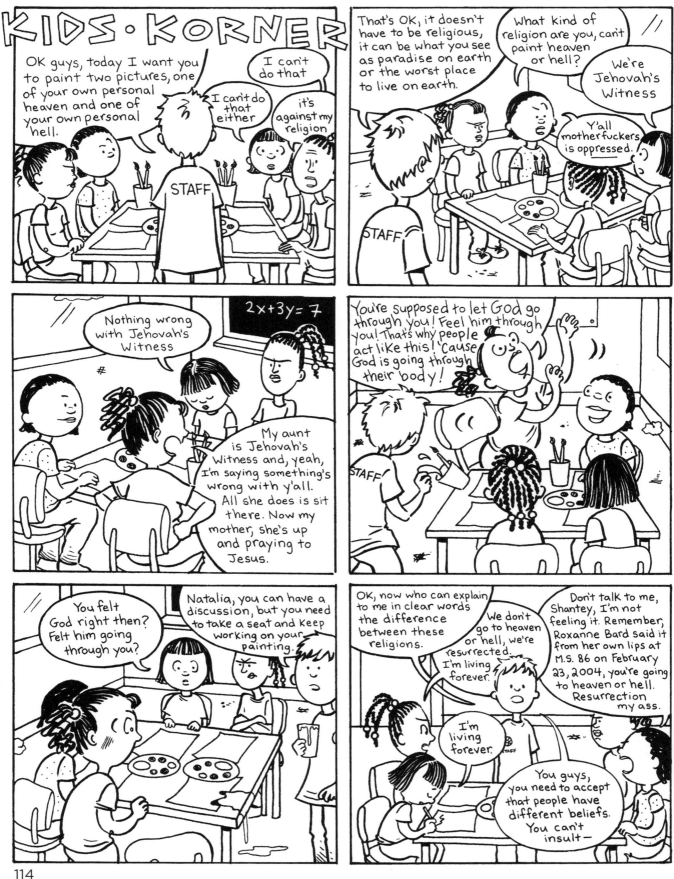

Ms. A, I don't mean to be disrespectful, but do you believe in anything?
I... believe in things.
I'm not scared of anyone, not even God.
well, you're stupid then.
I wish I could be in your shoes and just die for a day to see how it feels.
I believe in, uh, "a greater order."
I can say anything I want.
You think you can just do what you want, like you hit me with your belt in the lunch room.
I never did that!
Or, uh, fate. No. I believe in...
GOD STRIKE THIS GIRL DOWN!
But! I...
Wait, what do I believe in again?
I just realized I'm arguing with a little kid. How old are you?
I'm 13.
you're 13?
I'm 11.
Ms. A? I'm done.

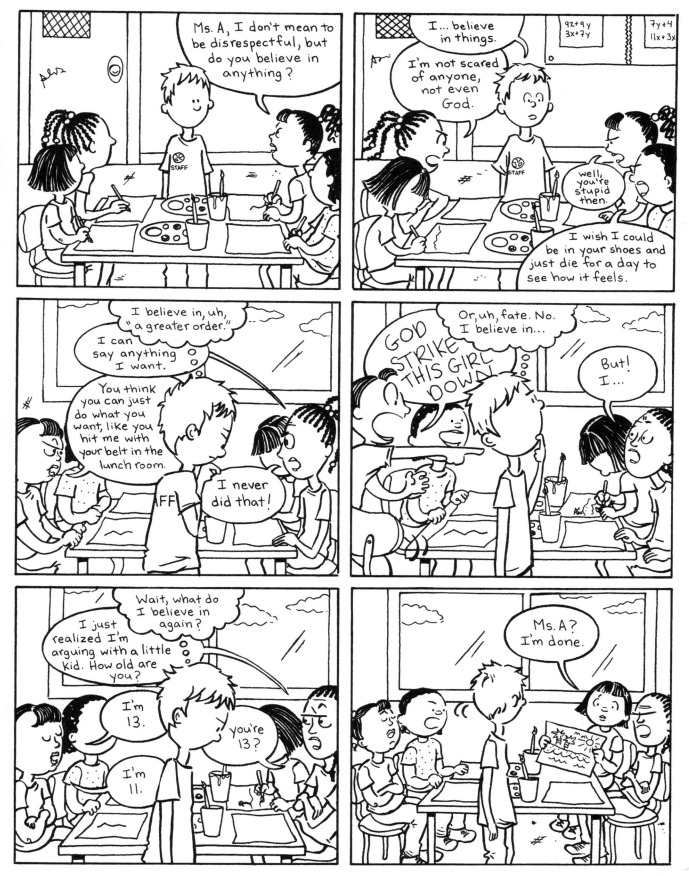

Kids Korner
Is that for fashion class today? I should be working on my lesson plans...
RE TR LO
Hm? No. I'm just making myself some pants.
RES TRU LOV
STAFF
I wonder if Roxanne is gay.
Good grief, I should not just be sitting around wondering which kids are gay. She's 11 for chrissakes. She's not gay.
STAFF
When Natalia and I grow up we're gonna live in the same house, in the same room, and have children together.
TRUTH LOVE
TRUTH LOVE

Kids★Korner
I called this staff meeting today to let you know how happy I am with all of your work. Everyone's been doing a fantastic job and I'm really proud of our team.
AFTER S
M.S. 86
STAFF
STA
I also wanted to share some big news, which is that I just found out I've been accepted into a program that will allow me to pursue my dream of becoming a personal trainer, so as of today I am no longer Director of After School.
what the...
AFTER
M.S 86
you're kidding.
STAFF
STA
Now there's no time to find a replacement, so effective tomorrow, Ms. Thomas and Ms. A will be in charge of the entire program as Co-Directors together. The two of you will be given 5 extra hours per week and a raise from 9 to 12 dollars an hour.
AFF
Do we need any more info, or...
Oops! I've got to run, I have class.
5 more hours per week at $12 per hour, equals... I'm rich! RICH! $ $!!
TER SCHO
I guess we're the bosses now.
AFTER SCHO
M.S. 86

Kids Korner
Now that I'm the boss I can teach whatever I want, whenever I want... I can... Girls Club. Oh my god. With no supervision I can teach any kind of Girls Club I want! Fuck this Abstinence Only shit. Girls Club is going ROGUE!
OK! So Girls Club is going to be a little different from now on. First off, I want everyone to study these sheets. We'll have our first test next week.
vagina facts
THE VAGINA
THE VAGINA
clitoris
clitoral hood
urethra
vagina
outer labia
anus
hee hee, "the clitoris is for female pleasure."
Why you laughing? That's a good thing. Stupidass.
DIFFERENT KINDS OF SEX
1.Oral
2.Anal
3.Manual
4.Toys
5. Interco
This is going so well!!
Now we'll have weekly tests, but the main focus of Girls Club will be YOU. All class discussion will revolve around answers to the questions you put in the Question Box. Here's a handout of the first answers I wrote last night.
So, the first question, which I think is a great kickoff, is: "Why don't men and women have the same private parts?"
Most men have penises and most women have vaginas, although some people are intersex, which means they have some combination of male and female genitalia, and some people are transsexual, which means the gender they were born with doesn't match the gender they identify with, so a man could have a vagina and a woman could have a penis.
huh.
Cool!

However, the reason most men and women have different genitalia is because the human species evolved so that males and females would be able to reproduce. Different animals in the world reproduce in different ways; some animals reproduce without having sex, other animals reproduce by having sex but have the same genitalia, and some animals, like humans, reproduce by males and females having different genitalia.
difference between male and female babies is that have XY chromosomes and females have XX chrom first few weeks of life inside a mother's uterus all babies have female genitalia, if the baby is born has XY chromosomes then a gene on the Y chromos called testis-determin factor is activated causes the hormone tes erone to be released baby's body. Testosterone a penis to grow and other physical differences throughout the life cycle. Female ovaries and adrenal glands produce testosterone but not as much.
EWORK
Uh, any questions?
STAFF
Vanessa!
AFF
what time is Dance?
TAFF

Kids Korner
OK, let's take it from the top, Dorothy and Scarecrow, in your places. Remember, we only have four weeks till the End of the Year Performance.
I wanna be Dorothy
THE WIZ
STAFF
Watcha working on?
No, I Know Scarecrows can't talk
Hey, honey! You got any spare change?
a story.
I was just on my way to pick up my kids when I saw it the sun dropped from the sky and all turned blood red and the people were pouring from the cars and beating the ground and praising someone. "Mom!" "Shut up Lonnie I want to tell her' "Stop it!" Said Nazihah. That's me, I'm 39 years old and this is the day I learned folks can raise from the dead.
Roxanne, this is amazing!
TRUTH
Anytime you want to work on it you can come here and use the computer in the office, OK?
OK, I gotta get to Fashion.
Next Day
BRIIINNGG
Bye Ms.A
Bye Missae
Bye!
FILES

My parent's gonna be late picking me up so I'll just work on my story.
OK
STAFF
FILE
tap tap
TAFF
tap_tap
YAWwn. I'm tired. It's OK if I lie down?
uh, sure
BRUUNGGGG
little sleepers! get back to work. I'm going to get some lunch, are you staying here?
uh huh
BIOLOGY
CAMPBELL

Kids Korner
Hey Ms. A, you Know 50 Cent?
I want chocolate milk
I wanna white milk
Ooooh you racist
yeah
I read in the paper it says he likes lesbian womens.
Well, that's too bad for him, right? 'Cause they don't like him.
What? They said he likes lesbian womens!
I Know, so, like, that's too bad for him, 'cause...
Ms. A. You need to stop wearing your hair like you depressed.
She needs a makeover.
Mr. W, you Know 50 Cent?
No, I don't "Know" 50 Cent.
Yeah! Can we give you a makeover?
Whenever I wear makeup I just look like a drag queen. I mean, not that that's bad. Wait, forget I just said that.
so we can?
uh, sure.
We need to start planning! FINALLY After School is actually FUN!!

Kids Korner
I'm writing a list of everything you need to buy for the makeover.
Now Ms. A, when we're done you gotta go out to a club. You got a drivers license?
Uh, no, I don't drive.
I could get my parent up in here and you could use her I.D.
Oh, no, I have an I.D. I'm over 21...
You own any tight blue jeans, Ms. A?
You need to get extensions. You know where to get extensions?
I saw a clip-on ponytail at the drugstore once.
MATH
STAFF
Hahahaha hahaha
heh heh
Here's the list. You can get all this by tomorrow?
And then she say...
Oooh! she didn't
OK
ONLY me and Natalia get to do the makeover.

KIDS KORNER
OK, so today's class is on "transformation." Natalia and Roxanne will be performing a makeover on, ah, me and the rest of you will paint Before and After pictures.
We're gonna prove it's no drag queen.
You need to sit up and cross your legs like this.
You want people to look at you and say, "Damn, she got a fatty."
I like Caucasian hair.
We wanna be like white people, but white people wanna be like us, white girls always want a big butt and big lips. You ready, Ms. A?
uh huh
ooooh!
You look like you got a boyfriend!
How come I can't help?!
OK, but only Shantey.
Shantey can do a little.

You're doing her hair like a little Jewish girl.
Well, I am half Jewish.
It looks good.
Mmm OK
Ellen, you laugh and I'm gonna shit on you, I'm gonna shit on you till you cry.
Let it burn Let it burn Gotta let it burn
Now Ms. A, you going out tonight?
uh, sure.
where?
A club in the city.
SLAP
Ms. A, if someone asks who did this, say kids did it. Don't lie. OK?
RIIIINGG
Bye
Bye Ms. A
Bye Ms. A
STAFF

341
STAF
TAFF
AFF
TAFF

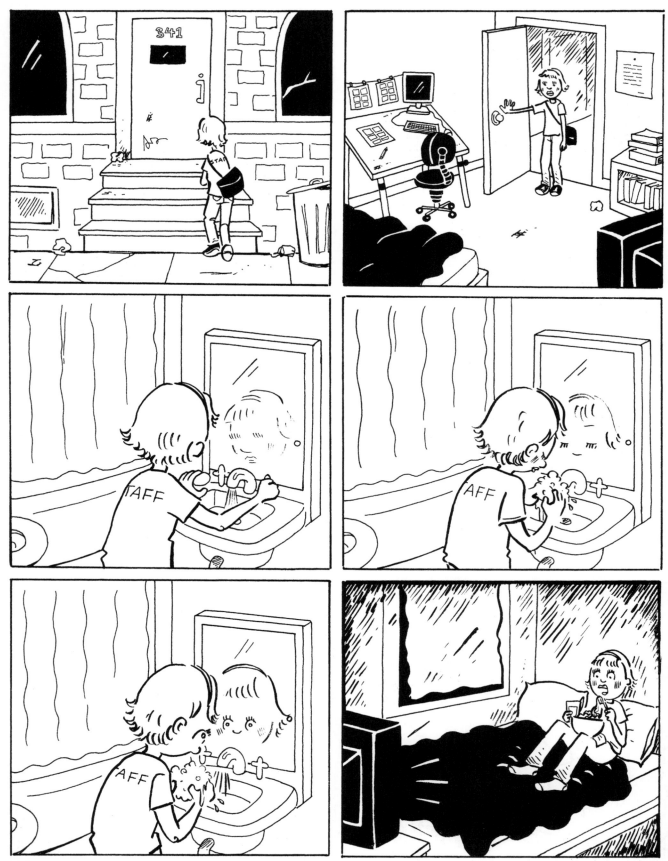

Kids Korner
Q: What does "cherry popped" mean? A: "Cherry popped" refers to the first time someone - generally a female- has sexual intercourse with a penis. The word "cherry" is used
Q BOX
I just had my 39th birthday and am going through a whole new experiences, repent time and forgiveness. My children think I work at the diner but really I stay at home with my potions.
I'm taking this stuff to the gym.
OK.
STAFF
Q BOX
STAFF
Clickety clackety
Q BOX
STAFF
you are so beautiful.
Q BOX
STAFF
3x+7y 8
uh... thank you.
you never heard me say that before?
No
STAFF
You know I'm gay, right?
really?
I never told you before, I have to keep it a secret from Natalia.
why?
STAFF

She'll think I like her. Like say I was to like you, she'd say that was disgusting.
well, I think if Natalia is your friend, then-
wanna know something else?
yes?
Q BOX
STAFF
$9x+2$ $3x+7y$
My name's not Roxanne.
what's your name?
Nazihah.
STAFF
Q BOX
STAFF
tell her
Q BOX
STAFF
Roxanne's real name is Nazihah.
MAY
Mmhmm
tell her the other thing
AFTER SCHO
M.S. 86
Roxanne is gay.
MAY
Mmhmm
Q BOX
FF
AFTER SCHOOL

I told her if Natalia-
MY NAME'S NOT NAZIHAH! I'M NOT GAY! I'M JUST PLAYING
I think Natalia might be gay though...
I'm not prejudiced, I just don't like gay people.
that's prejudice.
Anyway, I gotta go, my parent is waiting
She came out to me!
AFTER SCHOOL
M.S. 36

KIDS KORNER
Last Day of School
The vans will be here to take us to the event center soon, so make sure you have all your costumes.
Some of your parents will be there, and people giving money will be there, but don't be nervous. Dance and Fashion, you guys are ready.
And Drama, we may only have the first scene of "The Wiz" done, but it's going to be AMAZING!
No, I Know scarecrows can't talk.
Hey, honey! You got any spare change?
I was just on my way to pick up my kids when I saw it, the sun dropped from the sky and all turned blood red.

FASHION
HEAVEN D HELL
C'mon, everyone! The vans are leaving!
This lady told me how impressive the dancing was and I took all the credit myself!!
Ms. A, you gonna make sure we all get home safe?
uh huh
I've never felt so much love in my life. Why would anyone want to do anything else?

Want to come sit up front?
OK
I was hoping to drop you off last. If you weren't I was going to do it anyway.
I live at 341 south 4th street in Williamsburg.
please don't rape me
Where are we going? Is this even the way home? Please don't rape me please don't rape me
please don't rape me please don't rape me please don't rape me please don't rape me
What's the chance we see each other again?
I don't think so.
you sure?
yeah.
341
SHUT

Kids Korner
NEXT YEAR
Julie, the new Director, great to meet you.
you too
the reign has ended.
Hey! Roxanne!! You coming to After School?
WELCOME
STAFF
I'm not in After School, I'm doing tutoring. Gotta get my math down pat.
But what about writing?
I'm not in After School.
WELCOME TO
This After School?
I'm signing up for Dance 'n' Art!
me too!
fuck After School

Dyke March
2005 age 25

DYKE MARCH
5:30 PM
Meet Lou at BART
this sweatshirt's too hot
should I wear this hat?
I should have left it at home
does the color clash with my shirt?
my backpack's too heavy
what if I take my sweater off?
6:00 PM
Text girlfriend in New York
chick magnet
I want to french
6:30 PM
Down bottle of tequila
we come together as WOMEN
ROAR!
7:00 PM
Think Big
you know rich lesbians?!
we wanna meet rich lesbians!
they'll totally buy us dinner!
I want lobster and oysters on the half shell and...
7:30 PM
Paranoid Delusions
I think I see my ex I think I see my ex I think I see my ex I think I see my ex I think
8:00 PM
Girl from High School
'sup Ariel
it's Tiffany
BABY
8:30 PM
Follow around dancing topless girl who everyone wants to take pictures with
she's filled with the spirit of life.
fascinating

9:00 PM
Take picture with dancing topless girl
I am a tourist.
9:30 PM
Existential Crisis
CASTRO
10:00 PM
Use rich fag's bathroom
the line's over there.
thanks
10:30 PM
Get high
it was 4th grade.
and it was raining so we were watching a movie indoors.
something about a farm.
and a goat walking up a hill.
and I wanted to die.
So traumatized by sadness I blocked the rest out.
We have to find it
11:00 PM
Stare at the world's smallest penis
11:30 PM
Black Hawk Down
my phone!
12:00 AM
Gorge
12:30 AM
Head home, text girlfriend
didyouthat girlibjx?m qzdwlbrz*
1:00 AM
Pass out in Lou's brother's bed.
"RISKE"

The Chosen

2006 age 26

The Chosen

I was moving out of my apartment in Brooklyn, so I called the landlord to see about someone else taking over the lease. Within an hour, about five different Hasidic brokers were calling me, all wanting to be the one to show the apartment.

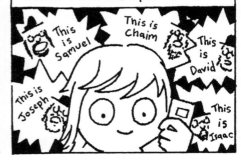

The first broker to come by I did not like at all. He brushed right past me, charged into all the rooms, and demanded I give him a copy of the keys so he could show the apartment whenever he wanted.

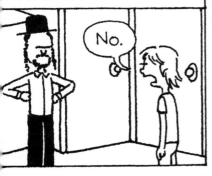

No.

The second broker, however, was different. He introduced himself (Joseph) and politely asked if he could see each room.

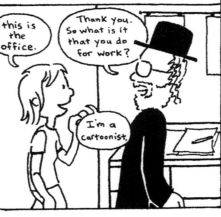

this is the office.

Thank you. So what is it that you do for work?

I'm a cartoonist.

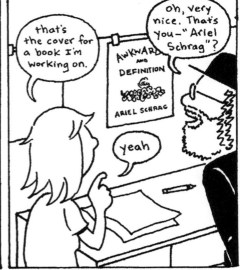

that's the cover for a book I'm working on.

Oh, very nice. That's you—"Ariel Schrag"?

AWKWARD AND DEFINITION
ARIEL SCHRAG

yeah

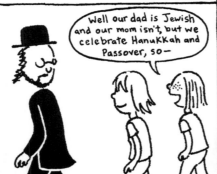

Are you Jewish?

ARIEL SCHRAG

The last time I'd been asked this question was by the Hasidic broker who first rented the apartment to me and my sister. At that point, she answered for us.

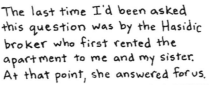

Well our dad is Jewish and our mom isn't, but we celebrate Hanukkah and Passover, so—

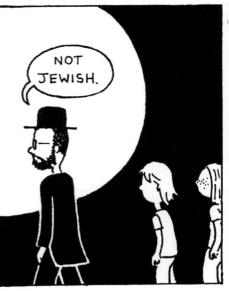

NOT JEWISH.

I liked Joseph. And I wanted him to like me. So this time I answered:
yes.
As he inspected the rest of the apartment I realized how "Jewish" I actually seemed. Almost all my stuff was packed up in boxes, but for some random reason two of the only items left out were:
1. A Menorah (FYI: it was July)
beautiful!
2. A 7-month-old HanuKKah greeting card
Is this family?
uh huh
very nice
Normally, neither of these would have been visible under the usual clutter of stuff, but I ignored this fact as my whole body tingled with the narcotic feeling of belonging.
Over the next week, Joseph showed the apartment several times. I gave him a set of Keys, but he always called beforehand.
This is Ariel, she's a wonderful artist.
Hi Ariel, it's Joseph. Hope you're well. Just wanted to see if I could show the apartment this Sunday. Shabbat Shalom.
One day, my friend Sam came over and I told her all about the Menorah and the HanuKKah card and how much Joseph loved me for being Jewish.
And you're not even really Jewish!
but... yes I am...
Real Jew.
A while later she came out of the bathroom, laughing.
So Ariel, nice toothbrush.
huh?
you just REALLY want to get this apartment rented, don't you?
I had completely forgotten about the ridiculous toothbrush my girlfriend had bought me and was horrified that Joseph had seen it. Did he think I'd PURPOSELY PLANTED these items in the apartment to TRICK him into liking me? The toothbrush's absurdity seemed proof that I WASN'T REALLY JEWISH. Had Joseph's image of me been shattered?
I never did find out. The next day, Joseph left a message that the apartment had been rented. I couldn't help but notice that he did not say, "Shalom."
But no matter what, for at least those two weeks, I had been one of The Chosen.

The Experiment
2006 age 26

THE EXPERIMENT
I live on Venice Beach in a hotel.
NO SMOKING
Outside, there is the faint, 24/7 sound of a drum circle.
a ratatat tat bop bee bop ba bum bum be bop ba bum bum ba bummm
The vague, constant waft of patchouli incense.
And when I peek through the blinds, this is what I see:
I make $5,006 a week writing for television.
When I take a bath, it feels like this:

For the past couple weeks, the writers' meetings have been on hiatus, so I'm not even really working. But I still get paid.
It makes me feel both ecstatic and incredibly anxious. Like I'm constantly procrastinating something that doesn't exist.
So far, I've spent most of my time driving back to the Santa Monica shopping area near work, buying clothes, returning clothes, and hiding out in my room.
I'm starting to feel bored, antsy, cabin feverish, and ill. Why don't I have any friends in this city? My friend Sam came from New York for a brief visit a week ago, but now she's gone and I can feel myself beginning to disappear.
It's nonsense! Nonsense! I'm in Venice Beach, at the heart of a vibrant community! What am I doing shut away in my room?!
I should embrace Venice for what it is and go out and join the people.
Which means, of course, that first I will have to get high.
My mom visited a while ago and brought pot with her. At first I was like, "Mo-o-om." But now I can put it to use.
There's No Smoking in the hotel room, so I put on The Beach Boys, open the window in the bathroom, and smoke in the tub.
the warmth of the sun
I feel cool and rebellious.

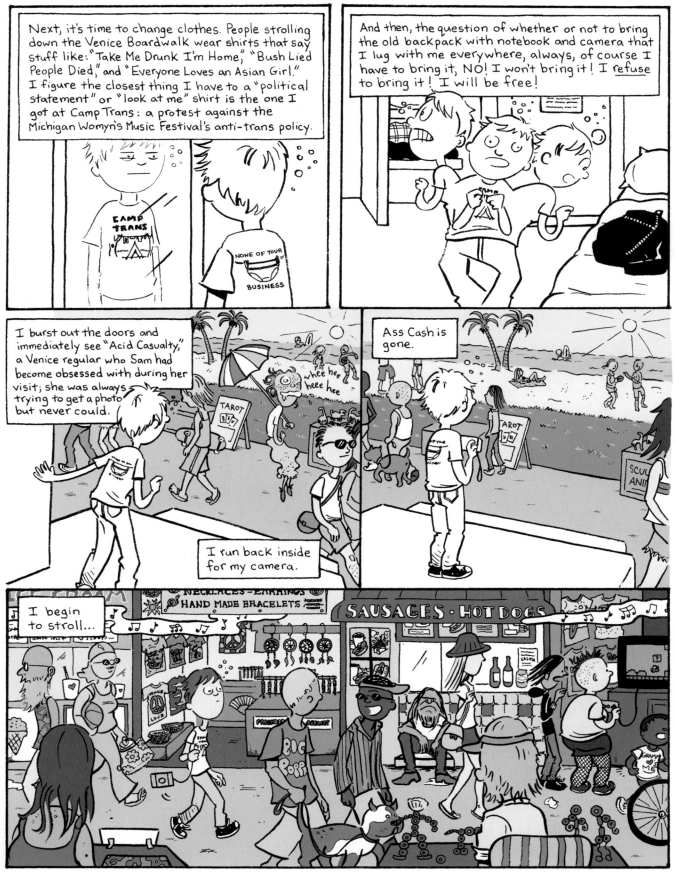

Next, it's time to change clothes. People strolling down the Venice Boardwalk wear shirts that say stuff like: "Take Me Drunk I'm Home," "Bush Lied People Died," and "Everyone Loves an Asian Girl." I figure the closest thing I have to a "political statement" or "look at me" shirt is the one I got at Camp Trans: a protest against the Michigan Womyn's Music Festival's anti-trans policy.

CAMP TRANS

NONE OF YOUR BUSINESS

And then, the question of whether or not to bring the old backpack with notebook and camera that I lug with me everywhere, always, of course I have to bring it, NO! I won't bring it! I refuse to bring it! I will be free!

I burst out the doors and immediately see "Acid Casualty," a Venice regular who Sam had become obsessed with during her visit; she was always trying to get a photo but never could.

whee hee heee hee

TAROT

I run back inside for my camera.

Ass Cash is gone.

TAROT

SCUL ANI

I begin to stroll...

NECKLACES - EARRINGS
HAND MADE BRACELETS

SAUSAGES · HOT DOGS

BIG POPP

Vegan Propaganda Man. No one can look away from pictures of slaughtered animals.
MEAT IS MURDER
END THE BLOODBATH
ANIMAL AUSCHWITZ
STOP THE MASSACRE
Circumcision Man. A strange calling in life. To sit every day on Venice Beach and educate about male circumcision/genital mutilation.
LEGALIZE FORESKIN
CIRCUMCISION
FORESKINS ARE NOT A BIRTH DEFECT
GENITAL INTEGRITY
The man who healed Britney Spears.
well it's like I told Britney...
HEALE
CHAKRA
PAIN · ILLNE
I decide it's time to get a smoothie. I go up to the stand and hover, choosing a flavor, when a gang of teenagers pushes me out of the way.
I want a smoothie I want a smoothie I want a smoothie I want a smoothie I want a smoothie I want a smooth
hee hee hee hee hee
hee hee hee
SMOOTH
Are they high? I sure am.
Blondes have more fun, see, look at all these blondes having so much fun.
Shut up you guys.
NONE OF YOUR BUSINESS
The teens sit down and I take a picture of them. Fortunately, since I'm invisible, they don't notice.
I pretend to take a photo of the scenery behind them, just in case.
shells... anyone want shells...
SNAP
SNAP
NONE OF YOUR BUSINESS
I buy my own smoothie and am on my way when—
PLANET CULTURE

Ass Cash. She's back. And has somehow changed into a new hip hop gear outfit. She's putting the outfit to use, dancing up a storm while a dude spins turntables. She's doing funky hip hop moves. Really getting down.
bee pop
SKrick
sKratch
Also enjoying the DJ are two girls, not dancing, but planted in front of his table, mesmerized.
...but how?
My body just knows what it's doing so I just let my imagination fly.
SNAP SNAP
A homeless-looking man carrying beer in a plastic bag joins, doing funky hip hop moves as well. A family watches as their baby boy dances. A woman grooves from the grass. The DJ has brought us all here, together.
beep skitch
sKratch
For me? N-no... thank you. Thank you.
I feel that I love him.
I keep walking.
PIERCING
2 For $9
hey sexy
WILL WORK 4 MARIJUANA
And decide to take some photos of myself. I don't care if I look crazy. This is Venice Beach. You're supposed to look crazy. I'm part of it.
SNAP

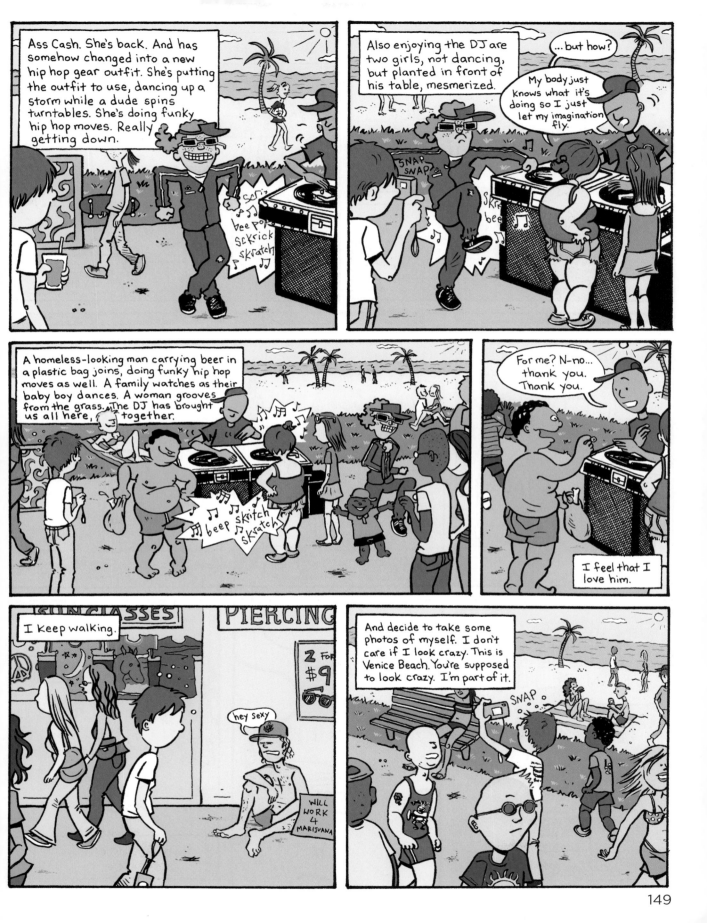

Next up is the skate park to troll for beautiful young skater boys. I find one who is perfect.
SNAP SNAP SNAP
CAMP TRANS
But feel a little conspicuous...
and am soon on my way.
"YOUR NAME on a GRAIN of RICE."
YOUR NAME
RICE
"YOUR NAME on a GRAIN of RICE."
CAMP TRANS
Why the fuck would anyone want their name on a grain of rice?
CAMP TRANS
WHO THE FUCK CARES IF SOMEONE CAN WRITE YOUR NAME ON A GRAIN OF RICE?!
CAMP TRANS
Laura
Conrad
Alice
I must get my girlfriend Kris her name on rice.
Both of our names on rice.

Uh, excuse me, do you know where —
Sue Ellen, customer
YOUR NAME ON A GRAIN OF RICE
ORIGINAL PAINT
yes, yes, yes, right here, Name on Rice?
hello
which one do you want?
um...
I moved to Venice back in the '60s and I've watched this place change...
When I first came here I'll tell you, my favorite people to talk to were the old Jewish people! I could sit and listen to them for hours. Especially the ones with numbers on their arms.
The first time I set foot on Vietnamese territory they were trying to kill me. That never happened before or after in my life, but in Vietnam they were trying to kill me. I lived half-minute to half-minute. Every day after I was out it was rat-a-tat-tat-tat. Of course the hypnosis cured me of most of that.
go ahead.
oh, um, this one.
write the name down here.
How old are you?
26.
No!! Hey, doesn't this look like a teenager to you?!
I can show you my ID...

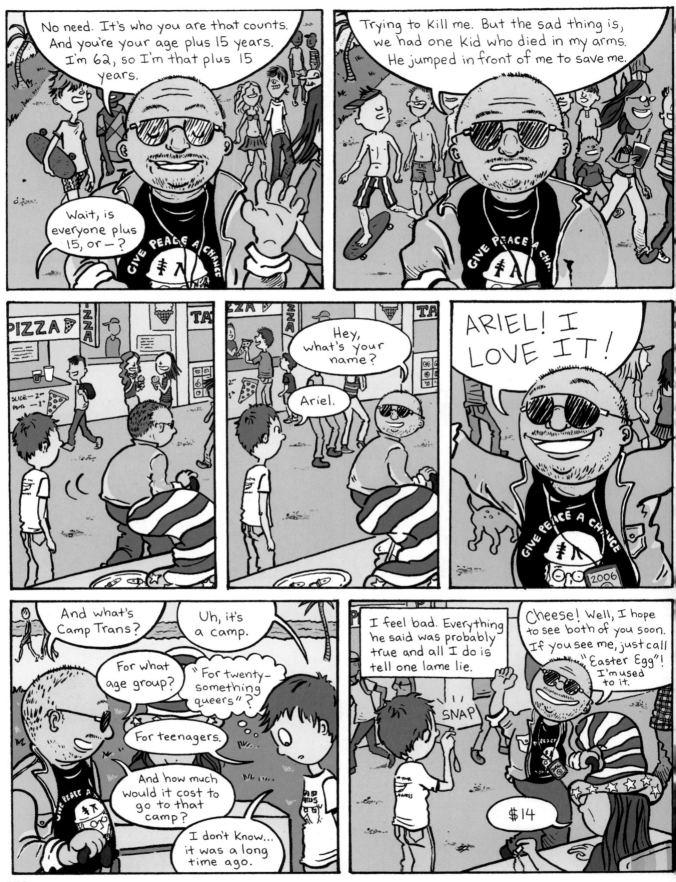

No need. It's who you are that counts. And you're your age plus 15 years. I'm 62, so I'm that plus 15 years.

Wait, is everyone plus 15, or —?

Trying to kill me. But the sad thing is, we had one kid who died in my arms. He jumped in front of me to save me.

Hey, what's your name?

Ariel.

ARIEL! I LOVE IT!

And what's Camp Trans?

Uh, it's a camp.

For what age group?

"For twenty-something queers"?

For teenagers.

And how much would it cost to go to that camp?

I don't know... it was a long time ago.

I feel bad. Everything he said was probably true and all I do is tell one lame lie.

SNAP

Cheese! Well, I hope to see both of you soon. If you see me, just call "Easter Egg"! I'm used to it.

$14

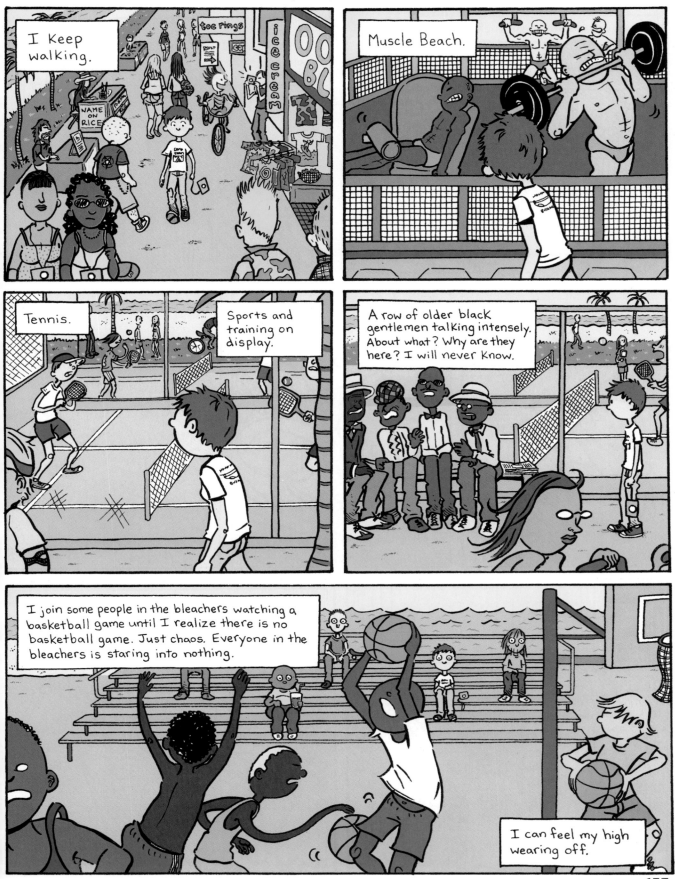

I keep walking.

Muscle Beach.

Tennis.

Sports and training on display.

A row of older black gentlemen talking intensely. About what? Why are they here? I will never know.

I join some people in the bleachers watching a basketball game until I realize there is no basketball game. Just chaos. Everyone in the bleachers is staring into nothing.

I can feel my high wearing off.

I turn around and head back. Pass a shirtless boy having some procedure performed on him. He seems naked, exposed, as if he's lost a bet and this is his punishment.
ORN DOG
ATM
Really he's getting a henna tattoo.
Boardwalk massage parlor. I burn with jealousy. I want that. I want someone to do that to me. But I can't.
SCIATICA NUMBNESS HEADACHE ARTH
THERAPY MASSAGE
NECK PAIN 20
FOOT 15
$15 CHAIR
$25 TABLE
$50 TA 1/2 HR
ATM
MASSAGE
Knead Knead
THUD THUD
DEEP TISSUE THERAPY MA
Aah! Aah! My shoulder! It's dislocated!
Drop the curtain! Drop the curtain! No one can see this!!
Someone call an ambulance!
ee ooo Weeooo We
SCIATICA NUMBNESS HEADACHE ARTHRITIS
DEEP TISSUE THERAPY MASSAGE
ACCEPT FAMILY & COMPANY PARTY
NUMBNESS, LEG $20
NECK PAIN $20
FOOT $15
$15 CHAIR
$25 TABLE
$50 TABLE
$40 NEC
ATM
SLAP
PUSH PUSH
NONE OF YOUR BUSINESS
Why is she giving a thumbs-up? Is it to let the massage guy know she particularly likes what he's doing? Or is it to let passersby know that she made the right choice deciding to get a massage on the Venice Boardwalk in front of everyone?
$25 TABLE
$50 TABLE
$40 NEC
SLAP
NONE OF YOUR BUSINESS

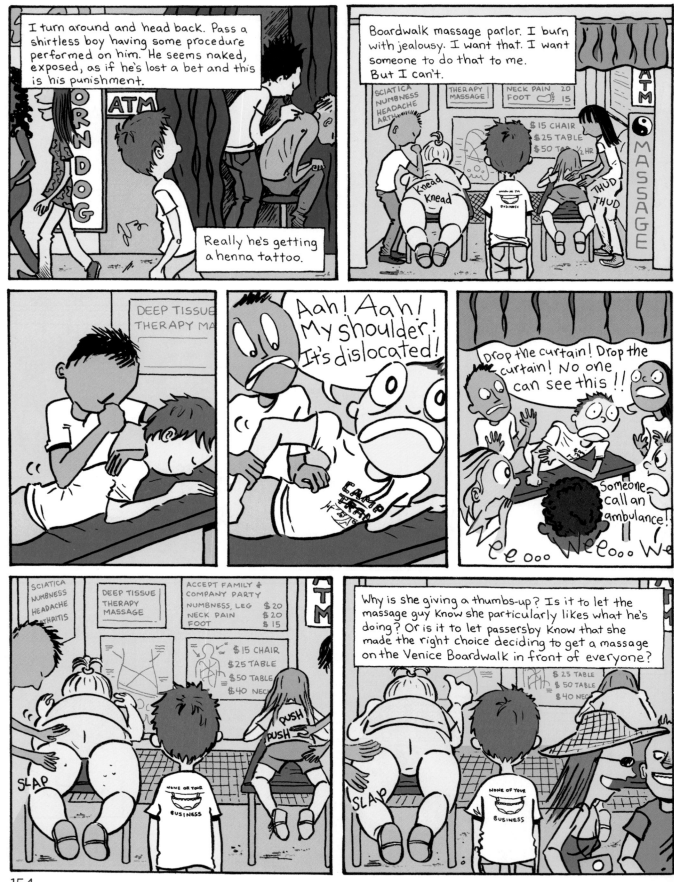

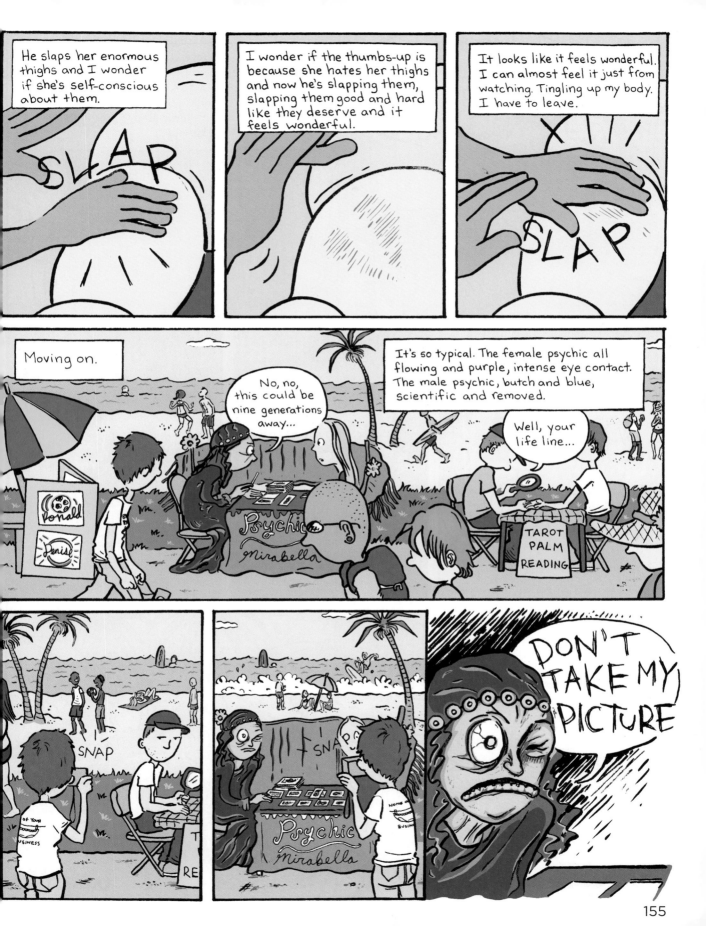

He slaps her enormous thighs and I wonder if she's self-conscious about them.

SLAP

I wonder if the thumbs-up is because she hates her thighs and now he's slapping them, slapping them good and hard like they deserve and it feels wonderful.

It looks like it feels wonderful. I can almost feel it just from watching. Tingling up my body. I have to leave.

SLAP

Moving on.

No, no, this could be nine generations away...

Psychic Mirabella

It's so typical. The female psychic all flowing and purple, intense eye contact. The male psychic, butch and blue, scientific and removed.

Well, your life line...

TAROT PALM READING

SNAP

SNAP

Psychic Mirabella

DON'T TAKE MY PICTURE

I get my picture taken ALL DAY, but not during a reading. NEVER when I'm reading.
Psychic
It's sort of wonderful how adamant she is. Venice people posing for their picture all over the place, me taking photos of everyone nonstop and no one giving a shit 'cause it's Venice. But this Psychic Lady, taking herself and her work seriously.
Psychic
T-Shirt $10
SMOKE
I'm sorry. I'll delete it.
I don't.
Now I have a hex on me.
The boardwalk has become crammed with people. I can barely move. The boardwalk, the boardwalk, it's closing in on me. I need to get home.

ICE CREAM
PIZZA
BOO.
HA HA HA
HA HA HA HA HA
HA HA HA
EEEEK!!!
ICE CREAM
PIZZA
why did the rooster cross the road?
AMAZING RAPPER $1
Get you butt o I'm
Yeah Man that's what they said when
HA HA HA
AMAZING RAPPE $1
I'm hungry I wanna
where is th
No
WHY ARE YO
MOM
VENICE SUITES
I make it back to my hotel room. The experiment complete.
NO SMOKING
It is cool. Calm. Quiet.
I feel so incredibly lonely.

Acknowledgments

Greatest thanks to my agent, Merrilee Heifetz, and my editor, Pilar Garcia-Brown. And to Lauren Wein.

Christopher Moisan, Beth Fuller, Dan Janeck, Stephanie Buschardt, and Liz Anderson.

To Molly Axtmann, Tania Schrag, Frederic Schrag, Julia Fuller, Toby Wincorn, Mel Plaut, Kris Peterson, Anna Sochynsky, Liz Brown, Melissa Anderson, Kevin Seccia, and Craig Webster.

Much of this book was worked on at the homes and in the company of Girls Comics: Gabrielle Bell, Lauren Weinstein, Karen Sneider, Julia Wertz, Julia Gfrörer, Liana Finck, and Tania Schrag.

To Sister Spit 2009: Michelle Tea, Beth Pickens, Sarah Adams, Beth Lisick, Ben McCoy, Rhiannon Argo, Kirya Traber, and Sara Seinberg.

Huge gratitude to RADAR Productions and the Corporation of Yaddo.

And for everything, every day, Charlie and Robbie.

My two biggest fears are...
1. Getting locked inside a public bathroom.
hum de dum
flusshh
wait. why won't this open? I'm turning it the right way. OK, I'll try the other way. Help! It's not opening! The lock is stuck! I'm trapped!
Dear God please just open! what am I supposed to do? Just start screaming from the bathroom? "Help! I'm in the bathroom!" MORTIFYING! Would anyone even hear?! oh my god I'm gonna DIE in this bathroom!
2. Having the door opened on me in a public bathroom.
did I remember to lock the door?
Oh! oh my god! I'm so sorry!
I'll just, ah, close the door here, sorry
I AM SO HUMILIATED DISASSOCIATING RIGHT NOW
I AM SO EMBARRASSED HAVING TO SEE YOU BE SO EMBARRASSED.
And that is basically the conundrum of life.